HOW TO ANSWER TOUGH QUESTIONS KIDS ASK

Doris Sanford

THOMAS NELSON PUBLISHERS

Nashville • Atlanta • London • Vancouver

Published in Nashville, Tennessee, by Thomas Nelson, Inc., Publishers, and distributed in Canada by Word Communications, Ltd., Richmond, British Columbia, and in the United Kingdom by Word (UK), Ltd., Milton Keynes, England.

Scripture quotations are from the *International Children's Bible, New Century Version,* copyright © 1986 by Sweet Publishing, Fort Worth, Texas 76137. Used by permission.

Library of Congress Cataloging-in-Publication Data

Sanford, Doris.
    How to answer tough questions kids ask / Doris Sanford.
       p. cm.
    Includes bibliographical references.
    ISBN 0-7852-8038-3
    1. Children—Religious life. 2. Child rearing—Miscellanea. 3. Parenting—Miscellanea. 4. Children's questions and answers. I. Title.
BV4571.2.S25 1995
248.8'45—dc20
                                                   94-48525
                                                   CIP

Printed in the United States of America

1 2 3 4 5 6 7 - 01 00 99 98 97 96 95

With love, this book is dedicated to
Elias Sanford Burch
my first grandson, who, being brighter than most babies,
is likely to ask very hard questions.
From, Grandma

CONTENTS

Medical Topics

Sexual Topics

Emotional Topics

Religious Topics

ACKNOWLEDGMENTS

Thank you to my secretary, Marilyn Gerhart, who has a knack for creating order out of chaos.

Thank you to Donna Johnson, who knows the Bible well enough to find the verses for each section and didn't bat an eye when I asked for Scripture dealing with gangs, Halloween, and organ transplants.

Thank you to Etta Wilson, my encourager and friend.

And thanks to the children who ask questions that deserve respectful answers.

HOW TO USE THIS BOOK

Children don't ask questions at the right time! When you are driving home exhausted, through heavy traffic with three neighbor children in the backseat of the car, they ask why people get drunk, or why some parents get divorced, or why the man in the tattered coat is shouting bad words at an empty park bench. It is enough initially to say, "Good question . . . I'm glad you asked." Most of the topics in this book can wait to be talked about until after the car is parked at home and parents can catch their breath and give focused attention to the child.

After a lifetime of professional work with children, both as a play therapist and now as a consultant to Children's Services Division, I have learned that the younger the child, the harder the questions. This book addresses those hard questions.

This is not a therapy book. This book supports parents in teaching a Christian worldview to inquisitive children who ask questions about "messy" problems in the world. Designed to be used as a quick reference, it is for Christian parents, teachers, child-care workers, Sunday school teachers, and others who hang out with kids, hear the questions, and need to "collect their thoughts" about a particular issue . . . in a hurry. It is not intended to be read from front to back in one sitting.

Each section provides general information about how and why children act as they do in particular situations; references for finding what the Bible says about the subject; and suggestions about what the adult might say to children from a Christian perspective.

Every suggestion won't work in every situation. Parents will need to select statements that seem to "fit" a particular child.

Comments offered for one situation might prove useful in other situations. For example, the child who has experienced the loss of a loved person by death, divorce, or illness will grieve. How the child lost the person is less important than the fact that the child cannot have the person they want and need.

Some children need professional therapy during major changes in their lives. Other children will do fine with the support of a loving adult. Decisions about therapy are usually based on extreme changes in the child's behavior or delays in normal development, not the particular event that occurred. When parents don't know whether a child needs professional help, they can ask the opinion of the school counselor, pediatrician, or another trusted adult who sees the child regularly. Finding a therapist who has expertise with a particular problem is more important than choosing therapists because they are Christian. When the parent calls a therapist, it is appropriate to ask how many children the therapist has treated with this problem, and what therapies are used with children, such as play therapy, medication, or family therapy.

At times children have difficulty expressing their questions. Knowing what other children have asked may help them formulate their own questions. Parents may want to invite children to tell what they have already heard about a topic before answering the question. A child's question may be simpler than the parent thought. At other times, parents may initiate the discussion when the timing seems right, for example, "Christians believe that abortion is wrong because . . ." Children feel strong when they have the facts about why the family believes as they do.

The answers offered in this book won't feel "right" for every family. Many sections present controversial issues about which Christians have a variety of viewpoints. Even so, it may help to look at one perspective, and clarify how your beliefs differ.

Children can't "tell by looking" at another person whether they are Christian. They need to interact with others and hear what they have to say, and then they need direction in developing a Christian worldview of social-political, medical, sexual, and religious issues. Because many of the issues are contemporary, there is no specific Scripture which addresses the problem by name. When that is the case, we have used scriptural principles which apply.

Some of the issues in this book will not directly affect the child; however, the child will be in school classrooms or on the playground with other children who are facing these problems in their families.

Children can develop a Christian worldview by learning to ask the right questions when faced with controversial issues:

1. Does the Bible say anything about this?

2. What was Jesus' example?

3. Are there basic guidelines in the Bible that apply to any difficult situation? (for example, to "pray about everything")

4. What is the advice of my parents? Grandparents?

5. Are there laws that apply to this situation?

6. How would my decision affect other people?

7. What does my church teach about this?

8. Would my decision make the world a better place or a worse place?

9. Do I have all the facts in order to make the best possible decision?

10. If there are other people involved, how will my decision affect them?

11. Is my choice likely to be successful? For example, if I donate my kidney for a transplant, what is the likelihood of the recipient living?

12. What have I learned from past experiences?

13. Would this decision allow another person to live longer?

14. Is this choice simply a matter of personal preference?

15. What is the age of the person involved?

16. How much will it cost and is the cost worth the money spent?

17. What do the people I most respect have to say?

18. What does common sense tell me is the right thing to do?

19. Are there rules I must obey because I belong to a club or attend a particular school?

20. What do people who know the most about this recommend?

The values and beliefs of parents are the single most important influence in determining the future beliefs of the child—like father like son. Children need to know that their parents rely on Scripture as the primary source of determining what is right and wrong, whether or not the answers seem correct in popular culture.

These are important issues. Parents make themselves available to hear the questions when they listen well and with respect. At times parents will not know how to answer the question. Children can accept, "I don't know" as an honest response. Sorting through the questions with the parent will help children learn to think for themselves.

A child's question doesn't have to be answered perfectly or thoroughly at the time it is asked. Giving one or two statements may be all the parent can offer at the time, or all that the child is ready to hear. All these topics can be discussed in bits and pieces again and again as the child grows. It is more important to welcome the question than to have all the answers. The child will have contact with other Christian adults, who can share the question. None of us parent alone. The traditional African saying, "It takes a whole village to raise a child" is true!

Doris Sanford, R.N., M.A.

Social Topics

ADOPTION

IT IS very difficult to keep an adoption secret. Children feel betrayed if they learn of the adoption from someone other than their parents, thinking, for example, *If my parents could withhold this information from me, what else are they not telling me?* Children should be told and they should be told by their parents.

What Children Might Experience:

- Preschool children may have a hard time understanding that they have two sets of parents. It is helpful for children to use different names for biological parents and adoptive parents, such as Dad for their adoptive father and Father for their birth father.

- Children who are adopted when they are older must develop sibling connections in the new family slowly. Questions about whether the parents love the biological children more are bound to occur.

- Adopted children overhear insensitive adult comments at times, such as "Why couldn't you have your own child?" These episodes should be handled with humor and a matter-of-fact statement, such as "He is our own child. Loving a child doesn't have anything to do with how he came into a family."

- Interracial adoptions bring unique challenges. Children need ongoing contact with children and adults of their race to establish their identity. The adoptive family can provide stories, music, and language instruction of the child's racial heritage and should celebrate holidays honored by that child's culture.

- Adopted children may develop unrealistic beliefs about their birth parents, such as that they are searching for the child, are beautiful, or are talented.

What Parents Can Do:

- Use the word *adoption* in casual, happy conversation while the child is two to three years old. For example, say, "We are so glad we adopted you."
- Tell the child he or she is adopted. Most authorities on adoption suggest early disclosure of the adoption. Those who advocate waiting until the child is older still suggest that the child's questions be answered honestly whenever they are asked.
- Repeat the story often. Telling a child about the adoption is never a single event. Children must be told again and again.
- Adopted children must address the question of why their biological parents did not keep them. This profound question should not be minimized by joyful parents who have adopted the child.
- Children need to know that nothing they did caused the adoption. For example, they should be reassured that they were not placed for adoption because they were "too much trouble."
- Convey your love and joy nonverbally. Smiling and hugging—nonverbal communication—are as important as the actual words you say. While you talk about adoption, show how pleased you are to have adopted the child.
- Define adoption in terms a child will understand. You might say: "You grew in another woman's body, but she was not able to take care of you. Maybe she had no money, or was too young, or she was not healthy. Your birth mother must have cared about you very much to be willing to let us adopt you and take care of you in a way she couldn't."
- Remember that the overwhelming majority of birth parents do love their children, even though they may not be able to adequately parent them.

What Parents Need to Know about Open Adoptions:

Open adoption is a matter of choice by birth and adoptive parents. It can occur in several ways.

- A face-to-face meeting to share medical and family background information is provided by the birth parents to the adoptive parents. Arrangements may be made for adoptive parents to be present at the delivery.
- Contact between the birth parents and the adoptive parents and child may continue as the child grows up.

Advantages of open adoption for children include:

- Children have less mourning to do because they do not lose their former family.
- Children know that their adoptive family accepts the reality of their biological family.
- Children are less inclined to develop fantasies about their biological parents when they have contact with them.
- The child has a large number of relatives to turn to.
- Children are more likely to understand that the reason they were placed for adoption is the birth parents' inability to provide care for them, rather than because the child was in some way at fault.

What to Avoid Saying in Talking about Adoption:

- Don't tell children that they were given away or taken away.
- Don't make negative comments about the birth parents. Part of the child's identity is attached to being their child.
- Don't tell children they are "special" because they were adopted. This may cause birth siblings to wonder if they are less special.
- Don't expect children (especially older children) to have only positive feelings about the adoption. Whatever the circumstances, the adopted child was separated from birth parents and may need to grieve that loss.
- Providing a "Life Story Book" that includes pictures and birth family information, medical data, stories about the child's birth, former pets, schools, medical doctors, and developmental milestones is helpful, especially for the older adopted child.

5

▶ WHAT THE BIBLE SAYS:

Galatians 4:6–7 And you are God's children. That is why God sent the Spirit of his Son into your hearts. The Spirit cries out, "Father, dear Father." . . . you are God's child, and God will give you what he promised, because you are his child.

Ephesians 1:5 And before the world was made, God decided to make us his own children through Jesus Christ. That was what he wanted and what pleased him.

▶ WHAT TO SAY:

"Your birth father must have had some wonderful qualities to have had a son like you."

"You can tell anyone about the adoption. Or, you may decide not to talk about it. The decision is yours."

"I don't know anything about your birth parents. I do know they gave us a wonderful daughter."

"I couldn't love you more if you had grown inside my uterus."

"Your mom and I chose to be your parents."

"You don't need to be embarrassed by your birth mother's behavior when she comes to visit. We accept her."

"I am your real dad."

"The adoption agency checked us out very carefully to be sure we would be good parents for you."

"We went to court with a lawyer and the judge made you legally ours. Then we had a major party!"

"I notice you are withdrawn after your birth mother visits. It is okay to love her and love us too."

"Love is something you decide. We have made a forever and ever promise to love you and take care of you."

"I like it when people say you look just like our family."

[Also see: Abortion, Premarital Sex]

ALCOHOLISM

What Children Might Experience:

ALCOHOLISM IS just as harmful to children as it is to the alcohol-abusing adult who lives in the home. Reassure children by telling them that in an average school classroom approximately one in five children will live with someone who abuses alcohol. It is a common problem and they are not alone.

Children can be told that some people are more sensitive to alcohol than others, but everyone chooses whether or not they will drink. We are responsible for our behavior even if we have inherited the potential to become alcoholics. Denial is a part of alcoholism. It is confusing for children to hear parents deny problems they know exist, for example, when they call a hangover the "flu."

It is natural for children to have simplistic answers to complex problems. They think, "Mom should just stop drinking." Children need to know that alcoholics cannot stop drinking without help.

- Children find a variety of ways to survive in an alcoholic home, such as taking care of the parent. Adopting survival roles requires giving up a normal childhood.
- Children cannot make an alcoholic parent stop drinking, but they can learn about the illness and how to cope with the stress of living with the alcoholic.

- Children from alcoholic homes may not learn how to express their feelings. They need help to learn to talk about how they feel.

What Parents Can Do:

The nonalcoholic parent is often just as emotionally sick as the alcoholic. Covering up for the alcoholic or trying to change the alcoholic doesn't work. The only person who can stop the drinking is the alcoholic her- or himself. A family that is preoccupied with alcohol may not be able to adequately parent the child.

- Tell the child that there is no such thing as an ex-alcoholic. When the alcoholic stops drinking, he or she is a sober alcoholic.
- Children need to know that it is never helpful to take sides when their parents fight.
- Help children figure out what to do in medical emergencies, such as when an alcoholic parent falls and hurts himself, or starts a fire by a lighted cigarette. Children should know how to call 911 or the police.
- Teach children to ride the bus system as soon as they are old enough to do so. This makes them less dependent on transportation from drinking parents.
- Read stories to the child about other children who live with alcoholic parents.

Discipline is frequently inconsistent for children in alcoholic homes. The child may be spanked for behavior that was ignored the previous day or praised for taking money from the kitchen piggy bank to buy milk for the family one day and scolded for the same behavior another day.

Children may believe they have some control over their parent's drinking by what they do or don't do. Children who grow up in alcoholic homes don't know what normal is. They need to know that other people have stress, but they are not alcoholics.

Children need to know that although some Christians drink alcohol:

1. Anyone who has a relative who is an alcoholic should not drink.

2. Alcohol takes away the ability to make good decisions.

3. Scripture teaches that being drunk is sinful.

4. Drinking alcohol makes a Christian vulnerable to other temptations.

▶ WHAT THE BIBLE SAYS:

Romans 14:21 It is better not to eat meat or drink wine or do anything that will cause your brother to sin.

Galatians 5:22 But the Spirit gives love, joy, peace, patience, kindness, goodness, faithfulness, gentleness, self-control.

▶ WHAT TO SAY:

"Once an alcoholic starts drinking, he can't control the amount of his drinking."

"You don't have to explain to anyone that your Mom is an alcoholic. You can tell your friends or not tell them. It's up to you."

"Nothing that you are doing causes your Mom to drink too much alcohol."

"Your grandfather isn't lying when he says he doesn't remember. Alcohol makes people have blackouts in their memory."

"It is never safe for you to get into a car with someone who has been drinking. Keep this quarter with you. You can call me or your grandma and we will pick you up."

"I think you must feel sad and mad and embarrassed that Daddy is an alcoholic. You don't need to pretend that it isn't a problem."

"You are right. It isn't fair that you have an alcoholic parent."

"I know that you love your grandpa. You can be mad at him and love him at the same time."

"You should not drink alcohol when you grow up since your dad is an alcoholic and you are at risk of getting the disease of alcoholism."

"Living with an alcoholic is hard. You deserve help."

"Even if Mommy doesn't stop drinking, you can learn to be happy."

"Write down the house rules when your mom is not drinking. Alcoholic parents forget what they have said."

"Any nine-year-old child would feel the same way."

"Can I give you a hug?"

[Also see: Drug Abuse; Parents Who Fight]

CAPITAL PUNISHMENT

What Children Need to Know:

CAPITAL PUNISHMENT is the planned, timed death of a person who has murdered someone. In the United States murder is the only crime that can result in punishment by death. There are usually several thousand people in prison in the United States who are on death row and sentenced to die, but only a few of them will actually be put to death in a year. It often takes five to ten years after a criminal is put in prison before he or she is put to death. About 75 percent of Americans believe that the death penalty should be used when criminals murder. Criminals are put to death in various ways in different states. Some methods of capital punishment include injection of a poison, inhaling toxic gas, hanging, electrocution, or by a firing squad.

Some People Do Not Support the Death Penalty Because:

1. The state is "doing the same thing" as the criminal by killing another person.

2. Capital punishment, they claim, does not result in less murder because criminals are usually not thinking about

the death penalty when they commit the crime, and criminals may be so emotionally involved in the crime that the consequences are not considered.

3. Capital punishment does not teach other people better ways of dealing with anger or solving disagreements.

4. Capital punishment may increase violence because it teaches that violence solves problems.

5. The damage has already been done by the crime and cannot be corrected by the death penalty.

6. Jesus taught that we should love and forgive people who have wronged us.

7. One of the Ten Commandments states, "You must not murder anyone."

Some People Support the Death Penalty Because:

1. It seems to be fair punishment for a person who killed someone else; in other words, it is a logical consequence.

2. It may prevent others from committing similar crimes.

3. The model set forth in the Old Testament of the Bible teaches that society should put a person to death for killing someone else—whoever kills a human being should be killed by a human being.

4. Capital punishment provides a sense of justice for the families of the person who was murdered.

▶ WHAT THE BIBLE SAYS:

Isaiah 26:10 An evil person will not learn to do good even if you show him kindness.

Colossians 3:25 But remember that anyone who does wrong will be punished for that wrong.

▶ WHAT TO SAY:

"God wants everyone to ask him for forgiveness for the wrongs they

have done, even people who murder someone. If they ask God to forgive them, he will."

"Being forgiven doesn't mean there are no logical consequences for committing a crime, just like saying you are sorry for breaking a glass doesn't mean that the glass isn't broken."

"Hurting someone because you are angry is never okay."

"We can pray for the people in prison, and we can send good books and Bibles for prisoners to read."

"Families of someone who has been murdered hurt for a long, long time. They hurt for years, maybe forever."

"Sometimes people blame the person who was murdered for being in the wrong place at the wrong time, but it is never the fault of the person who was murdered."

"Sometimes families of someone who was murdered believe that when the criminal is punished, the family will feel okay again, but usually they don't feel better."

"Learning peace-making skills is very important to our family."

"It is okay to feel sad that someone must die for their crime and at the same time believe that capital punishment is necessary."

"Violence is not fun, cute, or smart. It is dumb and wrong."

"Someday you may serve on a jury and have to decide whether someone will receive capital punishment."

[Also see: Murder]

CHEATING

BY THE time children are in junior high school, they will probably observe cheating at school every day. In some math classes, nearly all of the children cheat on tests. The majority of junior and senior high school students with B averages or better state they have cheated.

What Parents Need to Know:

The most common form of cheating at school is copying another student's homework. Other methods of school cheating include using hidden notes to pass exams, reading book summaries rather than the book, and copying work from books for essays without giving credit to the author. Some children cheat to get good grades, but many cheat because they are too lazy to do the work. For others, cheating is simply a well-established habit, done with little thought.

Children are more inclined to begin cheating when they observe adults cheat routinely in sports scores, taxes, or in lying about who is at home when an unwanted phone call comes. Cheating is less likely to occur in classrooms with a clearly stated intolerance for cheating; when there is a high student-teacher ratio; when work is screened for possible cheating; or when children are provided good models by adults who consistently are honest, even when it would be easier to cheat.

Children need to understand that it is not possible to cheat without stealing—taking credit for work they have not done—and lying—implying something that is not true. Children are exposed to dishonest behavior as a common part of growing up, according to *USA Today,* November 13, 1992:

- One-third of high school students state they have stolen something from a store within the past year.
- One-third admit to lying on an application form.
- Two-thirds acknowledge that they cheat at school.

Telling children that "honesty is the best policy" may be met with skepticism, since those who cheat seem to succeed with far less effort than those who do not cheat. Children need to learn that they are expected to avoid cheating, not just avoid "getting caught."

What Parents Can Do:

- Tell children that you know how hard it is to avoid group pressure to cheat.
- Be clear about your expectations. Tell your child you will not be upset if they bring home honestly earned but poor grades when they have done the best they could.
- Tell your child about your own temptations to cheat and ask your child to pray for you that you will do what God wants you to do. Don't tell little white lies.
- Don't overreact with attacks on the child's character when you discover cheating, for example, by shouting "You're a cheater!" Cheating is a wrong behavior that can be forgiven and avoided in the future. Children should not be forced into behavior by a self-fulfilling prophecy.
- Examine possible motives for cheating, including acting in rebellion against parents or obtaining the attention they need, when they are caught. Other children have a poorly developed conscience and need professional counseling.
- Be realistic about your expectations of young children to avoid lying and cheating. Preschoolers do not always know the difference between what is true and what is make-believe. A preschooler does not know *why* dishonest behavior is bad.
- Look for patterns that invite cheating, such as if a child puts

off studying for tests or waits until the last minute to do necessary work for major assignments. Show alternatives to cheating.

▶ WHAT THE BIBLE SAYS:

Exodus 20:15-16   You must not steal. You must not tell lies about your neighbor in court.

Ephesians 4:25   So you must stop telling lies. Tell each other the truth because we all belong to each other in the same body.

Ephesians 4:28   If a person is stealing, he must stop stealing and start working. He must use his hands for doing something good. Then he will have something to share with those who are poor.

▶ WHAT TO SAY:

"I respect the way you plan ahead on doing your homework. I have lots to learn from you."

"It must be hard not to cheat when you see so many of your friends cheating. You make God happy."

"It is more important to do your own work than to get a perfect paper by copying the work of someone else."

"We won't be mad at you if you miss some of your spelling words on the test because we know that you have really tried to learn them."

"I think some kids think that looking good is more important than being good. It's not."

"You cheated and that was wrong. You need to admit this to the teacher, so I will drive you to school before classes begin tomorrow."

"When athletes use steroids, they are cheating others who develop their muscles by hard exercise."

"I like the way you are a good example to the others in your class."

"It will take awhile for others to trust you since you cheated, but you can earn their trust by always being honest. In time they will trust you again."

"It is hard to know what to do when you see a friend cheating. I know

you don't want him to be mad at you, but telling the teacher can be a way to help your friend stop doing something that is harmful."

"You need the right attitude when you report cheating. You should not just want to get somebody in trouble. God sees your heart."

"You could help your friend stop cheating by offering to study with her before the test."

DIVORCE

What Children Might Experience:

A PARENT'S divorce can be one of the most frightening events in the life of a child. Even when marriages are unhappy, most children wish their parents would stay together. Children may believe that difficult problems can be solved in simple ways if their parents would just try a little harder. Preparing children for the reality of divorce when there is no hope of saving the marriage will help them cope with the multiple changes that divorce brings.

Boys and girls often respond to divorce in quite different ways. Boys are more likely to act troubled at the time of the divorce than girls, but both may experience long-range difficulties such as lowered self-esteem and difficulty with making lasting commitments.

The children who have divorcing parents feel stressed because:

1. There may be a lack of support for them.

2. They may feel abandoned by relatives, especially if relatives take sides.

3. They can't control what is happening.

4. Major changes occur in their lifestyles.

5. They may experience a sudden increase in responsibility.

6. The foundations of their predictable world are shaken.

What Parents Can Do to Support the Child:

- Tell all the children at the same time while both parents are still living in the home.
- Don't blame either parent for the divorce. Simply state the facts.
- Reassure the children that they will always be cared for.
- Children will need to mourn, even if the family was unhappy or the parenting inadequate. Don't minimize their loss.
- All children in the family will not respond in the same way. Some reactions will be delayed.
- Reading stories about other children who have experienced divorce in the family helps children know that their feelings are normal.
- Invite children to ask questions.
- Develop a working relationship with the noncustodial parent regarding issues related to the children.
- Many children will talk to their friends, not their parents, about their feelings.
- Children can be told that God's plan for marriage is that a husband and wife live together until one of them dies, but that even when two people have failed to do what God asked, God can forgive them and help them as divorced parents.
- Children need to know that they will not always follow God's direction in their choices either, but that God will forgive them when they admit they have failed and ask for his forgiveness.

▶ WHAT THE BIBLE SAYS:

Malachi 2:16 The Lord God of Israel says, "I hate divorce. And I hate people who do cruel things as easily as they put on clothes," says the Lord of heaven's armies. So be careful. And do not break your trust.

Matthew 19:4-6 Jesus answered, "Surely you have read in the Scriptures: When God made the world, 'he made them male and female.' And God said, 'So a man will leave his father and mother and be united with his wife. And the two people will become one body.' So the two are not two, but one. God joined the two people together. No person should separate them."

▶ WHAT TO SAY:

"There is nothing that you did to cause the divorce and nothing you can do to fix the marriage."

"The reason we are getting a divorce is personal, but you should know that we have really tried to work out our problems."

"We both love you, and you still have a 'real' family even though your mom and I won't be living together."

"The next thing that is going to happen is . . ."

"Dad will not be living in this house. He will live in an apartment and you will be able to visit him on weekends."

"God loves us and will help us through this hard time."

"I know it is hard to concentrate at school. I will help you with your homework until you can manage it alone again."

"I like the way you are able to say how you feel about the divorce. I know this is hard for you. I also know that you are the kind of kid who can deal with hard problems."

"I will be talking to a grown-up about my feelings and problems. It is not your responsibility to help me."

"All of the house rules will stay the same at our house."

"You can tell your friends about the divorce if you want to."

[Also see: Living with a Single Parent; Parents Who Fight; Stepparent Families]

DRUG ABUSE

DON'T WAIT until you think your child might be using drugs to talk about drug abuse. Children in treatment for drug abuse often say that they used drugs for two or more years before their parents knew about it.

What Parents Can Do:

A close, loving family that has fun together is the greatest incentive for a child to stay away from drug use. Peer pressure is stronger than most children can admit, and a family that provides a happy, safe, stable place to be will counter the powerful tug of peer influence. Don't be afraid to be a strong parent and to state clearly what will happen if the child uses drugs. Children who have strong self-esteem will have a much easier time resisting peer pressure to try drugs.

Which drugs are currently being used and how these drugs physically affect children changes rapidly. Admit that you don't know about particular drugs. Offer to learn about them and seek outside help. By the time a child is eight years old, he or she should know what an illicit drug is, why it is illegal, what it looks like, and what harm it can do. The greatest risk for starting to smoke or use drugs comes in the sixth and seventh grades.

Children should know that TV advertisers try to persuade people to buy their products so they will make money, not because they want to help the consumer. This is also true of people who try to sell street drugs. Telling a twelve-year-old girl that she will get lung cancer by smoking is less likely to make an impression than telling her that her breath will stink.

Teach kids how to say No, to ask questions about an activity where drugs might be used, and to leave a situation in which they feel pressured to use drugs.

Know the signs of drug abuse in children:

- Red eyes; wearing sunglasses to hide eyes; changes in pupil size
- Runny nose
- Change in appetite, sleep patterns, and grooming
- Sudden need for more money; unexplained spending
- Mood changes
- Loss of interest in participating in sports
- New friends who are known drug users
- Sneaky behavior

The Bible doesn't teach directly about drug use, but there are biblical principles that apply. For example, Christians are taught not to do things that take control over them, and that God lives in the body of the Christian.

Children need practice saying No. Give them "let's pretend..." situations.

▶ WHAT THE BIBLE SAYS:

Proverbs 3:6-8 Remember the Lord in everything you do. And he will give you success. Don't depend on your own wisdom. Respect the Lord and refuse to do wrong. Then your body will be healthy. And your bones will be strong.

Romans 6:23 When someone sins, he earns what sin pays— death. But God gives us a free gift—life forever in Christ Jesus our Lord.

Romans 12:1-2 So brothers, since God has shown us great mercy, I beg you to offer your lives as a living sacrifice to him. Your offering must be only for God and pleasing to him. This is the spiritual way for you to worship. Do not change yourselves to be like the people of this world. But be changed within by a new way of thinking. Then you will be able to decide what God wants for you. And you will be able to know what is good and pleasing to God and what is perfect.

▶ WHAT TO SAY:

"In our family we don't allow the use of illegal drugs."

"I am very concerned about your friend Jeff's use of drugs."

"I trust you and saying No is hard, but because I love you, the answer remains No."

"When someone asks you to a party where drugs might be used, you can say:

- *'I'm doing something else that night.'*
- *'My parents would kill me.'*
- *'Why don't we go to a movie instead?'*
- *'Everyone is NOT doing it.'"*

"I would like to have a party for you and your friends at our house. Your friends are welcome to come over anytime when I am home."

"Real friends don't ask each other to do things they know are wrong."

"I want to know where you are and who you are with when you are away from home. If your plans change after you leave home, then you must phone home and tell your mom and me."

"If someone calls you a chicken for not using, you can say, 'I would be a chicken if I used drugs just to impress you.'"

"It is hard to say No to drugs when you are at a party and others are using. If you are in an uncomfortable situation, you can call home. We will be very proud of you and come to get you right away."

"What do you think would help you most to stay drug free?"

"If you use drugs or drink, you are grounded for three months except for school and church activities."

[Also see: Alcoholism]

EUTHANASIA

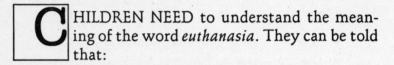

CHILDREN NEED to understand the meaning of the word *euthanasia*. They can be told that:

- Active euthanasia means causing the painless death of a person, usually one who has an incurable or terminal illness. *This is not legal in most states.*

- Passive euthanasia means doing nothing to prevent the death of a person by medical treatments, or withdrawing treatment once it is started when it is clear there is no hope of helping the person. *This is legal in the United States.*

The laws about euthanasia vary and are different in other countries. Children can be told that it is not always easy for the doctor to know when a person cannot be helped to get better. Doctors might have the ability to keep a person's heart beating and his lungs breathing even though the person's brain can no longer function.

What to Tell Children about Active Euthanasia:

- Children should be familiar with the language often used to describe active euthanasia, for example the phrases "the right to die," "death with dignity," and "mercy killing."

- People who support active euthanasia believe that people who want to die should be helped to die if they are unable or unwilling to do it themselves.

- Active euthanasia might be done by giving a person an overdose of drugs that will cause death, by giving poison, by leaving a gun at the bedside, or by other means.

- Active euthanasia is morally, legally, and spiritually wrong. It is murder.

What to Tell Children about Passive Euthanasia:

- Children can be told that it is possible for adults to leave instructions about what they would like done when and if they are unable to give the doctor directions, such as if they are unconscious. They can do this by

    1. *A Living Will* (also called a Directive to Physicians). This is a legal paper stating that if you have an incurable illness or injury, you do not want your life prolonged by extraordinary treatment, such as using a machine to make you breathe when you cannot breathe on your own.

    2. *Durable Power of Attorney.* This is a legal paper naming the person you would like to make the decisions about what to do for you when you aren't able to make your own decisions, for example, if you are in a coma.

- It is not against the law to refuse medical treatment or to give people medicine to keep them from having pain.

- It is not illegal to withhold or to withdraw life-support treatment even if the person is unconscious and unable to say what he or she wants done. Family members or the person responsible, along with the doctor, can make the decision.

▶ WHAT THE BIBLE SAYS:

Psalm 84:5 Happy are those whose strength comes from you.

Jeremiah 10:23 Lord, I know that a person's life doesn't really belong to him. No one can control his own life.

Matthew 5:21 You have heard that it was said to our people long ago, "You must not murder anyone. Anyone who murders another will be judged."

▶ WHAT TO SAY:

"Our family believes that God values human life, even if a person is unconscious. We do not believe in active euthanasia."

"Your mom and I have signed a durable power of attorney form because we would like Uncle Ken to make the decisions about what to do if we are unable to decide ourselves."

"God can teach people important lessons in difficult situations, such as how to comfort others."

"God has a purpose for our lives, including when we are suffering or dying."

"The doctors will not do CPR on Grandma if her heart stops because that is what we have decided, but she will be kept comfortable and given water if she can swallow and pain medicine if she needs it."

"Active euthanasia is wrong because:

- *There might be pressure on people to die so that they won't be a burden on others;*
- *It isn't always clear whether a person can be helped or not;*
- *And, people who want active euthanasia may change their mind after they are no longer depressed."*

[Also see: Suicide]

FUNERALS

CHILDREN CAN be told that a funeral or a memorial is a service that:

1. Honors the life of the person who died.

2. Helps family and friends begin the grieving process.

3. Acknowledges the reality of the death.

A *funeral* is a service where the body of a dead person is present and a *memorial* is a service without the body present. The choice about which service to have is often based on what is most familiar to the family.

Children may want to participate in the funeral by placing a drawing in the casket or by reading a poem in the service. Children often feel powerless after someone dies, and they need to know that they can help comfort people who are grieving.

What Children Need to Know:

Children are curious about the events following death and what will be done to the body. Procedures vary, but the following often take place.

- The funeral director is notified when a person dies and will come and get the body. The family chooses the funeral director that they want.

- There are laws requiring that something, such as cremation, embalming, or burial, be done to the body within twenty-four hours.

- *Embalming* means removing the blood and other body fluids from the body and replacing them with a disinfectant. This slows down the changes that occur in the body after death and prevents the body from becoming unsafe to the public.

- *Cremation* means placing a body into extreme heat, burning it until it becomes tiny bone fragments like coarse sand. An adult body weighs about five pounds after cremation. Cremation may be done in a special chamber called a *retort*. Children should know that it does not hurt to burn the body after a person is dead because a dead body has no feeling. The cremated remains may be placed in a special container called an *urn*, or they might be buried.

- *Burial* is usually at a cemetery. The family must buy a plot of land, and a gravedigger prepares a large hole where the casket will be placed. The family buys a marker to go on top of the grave so everyone will know the name of the person who is buried there.

- There may be *viewing* at the home or funeral home prior to the service so that people can see the body of the person who died.

- If there is a funeral, the funeral director washes the body, fixes the hair, and dresses the body in the clothes the family provides.

- The body might be buried in an above-ground vault.

- Funerals and memorials usually cost several thousand dollars. Immediate cremation without a funeral is less expensive.

- A notice will be put in the newspaper to inform people that the person has died and when the funeral will be. This is called an *obituary*.

- Flowers are given at a funeral to tell the family that the person was loved and will be missed. They are given to comfort the family.

▶ WHAT THE BIBLE SAYS:

Isaiah 25:8 But God will destroy death forever. The Lord God will wipe away every tear from every face.

1 Corinthians 15:54-57   "Death is destroyed forever in victory." "Death, where is your victory? Death, where is your power to hurt?" Death's power to hurt is sin. The power of sin is the law. But we thank God! He gives us the victory through our Lord Jesus Christ.

Psalm 23:4   Even if I walk through a very dark valley, I will not be afraid because you are with me. Your rod and your walking stick comfort me.

▶ WHAT TO SAY:

"Here is what will happen at the funeral . . ."

"You can go to the funeral if you want to go, or you can stay at home with a baby-sitter. You decide which you want to do."

"Sometimes the casket is opened at the end of the funeral and people walk by it. You don't have to do that if you don't want to."

"If you are uncomfortable or want to leave during the funeral, just tell me and I will go out with you."

"Some people may be crying at the funeral, but not crying doesn't mean that you didn't love the person just as much as the people who are crying."

"The body is the house that Grandpa lived in. The real Grandpa is in heaven. I think you will be able to tell that Grandpa has died when you see his body."

"Seeing a dead body might be scary. I will stay close to you and you can ask any questions that you want to ask."

"It makes the family feel good to know that we loved her and wanted to come to her funeral."

"A funeral service is something like a church service. There will be music and a talk."

"The family decides what they want to happen at the funeral. There are lots of choices they can make."

[Also see: Death of a Pet; Suicide]

GANGS

What Children Might Experience:

IDENTIFICATION WITH a gang doesn't happen overnight. Pre-gang behavior begins in grade school, not junior high. The decision to join a gang is often made by the fifth grade. Some children who become gang members are from families that are financially poor. The children may see gang membership as a source of income from such things as drug dealing and stealing. Some children seek gang membership because they want to belong to a "family." The majority of gang members come from single parent homes. Some of these families have chaotic lifestyles with few controls. Gang membership provides a code of rules the child must obey. Rules provide security. Boys who lack male role models at home may seek a gang which emphasizes masculinity. Girls may join because their boyfriends are gang members or because they seek the sense of belonging that gang membership provides.

Perhaps the strongest reason children join gangs is pressure from peers. A child may join simply to be accepted. Or children may join as a matter of survival.

You Can Decrease "Wannabes" By:

- Building genuine self-esteem in the child

- Providing good male role models
- Giving attention and praise for positive behavior
- Teaching children how to say No

What Children Need to Know:

Name the gang activity using the correct language. Tell children that taking a car for a joy ride is auto theft and buying marijuana is possession of a controlled substance.

Tell children that joining a gang usually means being involved in drugs and alcohol; destroying property with graffiti and vandalism; endangering the lives of their families; ruining their chances of becoming somebody when they grow up; and, often, ending up in prison or dead.

Be sure that children understand that many gang activities are against the law, such as carrying a weapon, selling drugs, and destroying property.

Learn gang clothing colors in your community, i.e., a local gang might wear blue baseball caps, or red scarves to identify themselves. Children should avoid any hint of gang affiliation in their dress.

▶ WHAT THE BIBLE SAYS:

Proverbs 1:10-11, 13-15 My child, sinners will try to lead you into sin. But do not follow them. They might say, "Come with us. Let's ambush and kill someone. Let's attack some harmless person just for fun. . . . We will take all kinds of valuable things. We will fill our houses with what we steal. Come join us, and we will share with you what we steal." My child, do not go along with them. Do not do what they do.

▶ WHAT TO SAY:

"A gang is a group of people who get together for a purpose and disobey the law in their activities."

"Our family does not approve of gangs. Please tell us if anyone asks you to join a gang. We will help you."

"Success and hard work go together."

"I'm so glad you belong in our family."

"See that gang graffiti. Someone will have to buy paint and take the time to paint over it. Graffiti hurts other people's property."

"Real friends never ask you to do anything that could hurt you."

"Why do you think people join gangs?"

"Some groups are good and some are bad. A gang is bad."

"How do you choose your friends? What qualities in a friend are important to you?"

"If someone in a gang approaches you, you can:

- *Keep your cool. Don't look scared.*
- *If the situation is not tense or frightening, be confident, friendly, and joke around if you can.*
- *Don't argue with anything they say.*
- *WALK, NOT RUN to the nearest helping adult or safe building. Running may indicate fear and challenge gang members to chase you.*
- *Don't walk alone in high-risk places."*

[Also see: How to Make Friends; Money; Murder]

How to Make Friends

ONE OF the most important skills a child learns in order to acquire sturdy emotional health throughout life is the ability to develop and maintain friendships. Making friends is clearly a learned skill and not an automatic process. Children need to be taught how to play and share with others; how to develop empathy by learning what other children feel; and how to resolve conflict when there is a difference of opinion.

The number of friends a child has is less important than the quality of friendships. Deep, lasting friendships with one or two other children are adequate to nurture the soul of a child. Even when children are very young, the presence of good friends can sustain them through stress in ways that adult relationships cannot. Children need the warm affection of peers and to be valued and accepted by other children.

Friends act as mirrors, helping children establish their identities. Friends provide feedback on what the child can do successfully and validation that the feelings the child has are shared by others—"I am like other kids my age."

Children Who Make Friends Easily:

- Pay attention to the words and actions of other children, and how they respond to situations.

- Care about the feelings of others.
- Are tactful and say nice things about others.
- Are affectionate, funny, and fun to be with.
- Are enthusiastic about activities.
- Take turns, share; allow others to decide when to end an activity.
- Are pleasantly assertive.
- Know how to make up after a disagreement.
- Have lots of ideas about fun things to do.

Children who live in stressful home situations may have little opportunity to observe and learn healthy friendship-building skills. By the time a child is in third grade, she should begin to develop friendships with children who are different from herself.

When a child enters junior high school, he is old enough to understand that friends change and grow in their own ways and that being "exactly alike" is neither necessary nor desirable for maintaining a relationship.

What Parents Can Do to Help Children Learn to Make Friends:

- Start by observing specific behaviors in the child which separate him from others. Why doesn't he have friends?
- Practice simple friend-building skills in role-play for ten minutes each day with an adult. Praise successes.
- Tell the child immediately when her behavior hinders the development of friendships, and tell her exactly what she can do to correct the problem.
- Teach specific, practical skills:
  1. Listen to others.
  2. Find something nice to say about someone else.
  3. Smile, say hello, and show interest in what others are doing.
  4. Remember others' names.

▶ WHAT THE BIBLE SAYS:

Proverbs 17:17 A friend loves you all the time.

Proverbs 27:10 Don't forget your friend or your father's friend.

Proverbs 27:17 Iron can sharpen iron. In the same way, people can help each other.

▶ WHAT TO SAY:

"I heard you tell Robbie that he is a great T-ball player. That will make him feel happy inside. Good friends tell each other what they do well."

"I liked the way you asked Eli what he wanted to play."

"Let's pray for a special friend for you. I know you are lonely."

"How about inviting Amanda over to help us make cookies this afternoon?"

"Ask Jesus to forgive you for arguing with Michael, and then tell Michael that you are sorry and want to be his friend again."

"I'm so glad you and Joel are friends. You choose nice kids to be your friends."

"Hannah just moved to our neighborhood, so I bet she needs a friend to play with."

"Jesus is the best friend of all. He never, ever, disappoints us."

"I know that you feel jealous when your friend plays with other kids. Real friends allow others to have freedom. Maybe it would help you to spend time with other friends also."

"Being God's friend means that you want to spend time with him, just like being Jena's friend means you want to be with her."

"It takes awhile to know if someone can keep a secret. It's smart to not tell big secrets right away until you know for sure if a friend can be trusted."

[Also see: Gangs; Self-esteem]

LIVING WITH A SINGLE PARENT
(AFTER A DIVORCE)

What Children Might Experience:

THE DIVORCE of parents is not a one-time event. Its effects linger on and on. Many children continue to feel rejected by the noncustodial parent. Half the children in post-divorce homes experience the continued fighting of their parents, often on topics that relate to the child such as financial needs, visitation, or vacation plans. Children sometimes overhear these conversations and feel guilty.

Although children may be proud to be trusted with new responsibilities in a single parent home, they may also feel abandoned. Children are sometimes left at home alone while their parent is at work; they may be asked to fix dinner or help with the care of younger siblings. Ninety-five percent of children have no consistent place for support and comfort following divorce. Signs of distress in young children frequently include nightmares, clinging, regression, crying, tantrums, being demanding, and manipulating (in an attempt to reunite the divorced parents).

Divorce changes the way kids understand God. A child who

could not trust a human father will have greater difficulty trusting the heavenly father. It helps to remind the child that God will never disappoint or leave us. Children who have regular contact with the noncustodial parent are emotionally healthier than those who do not.

What Parents Can Do:

- Expect the most of your child. Do not generalize the child's behavior on the divorce by assuming that *all* of the child's behavior is caused by the divorce. Your child can heal, just as you can heal.
- Help your child figure out ways to earn spending money if the divorce has caused financial stress.
- Seek out experiences for the child with other adults of the noncustodial parent's gender, for example a soccer coach or teacher.
- Understand that the issues related to the divorce will change as the child grows. They will not all be apparent in the beginning. Ask for advice from other successful single parents.
- Share your anger, hurt, and anxiety with an adult, not your children.
- Encourage play. Discourage assuming adult responsibilities or roles at home.
- Spend time with your child having fun. Make the children your number one priority. It will be worth your effort!

A Caring Friend Can Help By:

- Not taking sides. The child needs and wants both parents.
- Including the single parent family in your own family gatherings.
- Not judging. We don't know the whole story.
- Praying for wisdom about what to say and how to help.
- Spending time with the child playing and having fun. It is unnecessary to talk about the divorce each time you are together.
- Not giving unsolicited advice. Just listen and help the child consider options.

- Reassuring children that they will be able to have a successful marriage when they are grown.

▶ WHAT THE BIBLE SAYS:

1 Peter 4:12 My friends, do not be surprised at the painful things you are now suffering. These things are testing your faith. So do not think that something strange is happening to you.

1 Peter 4:19 So then those who suffer as God wants them to should trust their souls to him. God is the One who made them, and they can trust him. So they should continue to do what is right.

▶ WHAT TO SAY:

"I know that it is hard for you when I don't talk about your mom. Please ask the questions that you need answered."

"It must be hard for you when I have to go to meetings and you wish I could stay home with you."

"I yelled at you and you didn't deserve it. Sometimes I take my anger and hurt feelings out on you. Please forgive me. I will try not to do that."

"I know that you worry when I am crying. I can still take care of you even when I feel bad. And, I won't always feel sad."

"You don't have to be embarrassed to tell your friends about the divorce. You didn't do anything wrong."

"Let's see if you could be in a Sunday school classroom with a male teacher. I know you need to be around good men."

"I know that you are worried about us not having much money, but that is something we can pray about. God will help us."

"I am sorry to hear that your mom said those things about me. I hope you don't believe that they are true."

"You don't need to sleep in my bed with me. You are safe in your own bed, just as you always have been."

"I know that you are unhappy about my dating another woman, but the decision to date is a grown-up decision, not a child's decision."

"Going to court does not mean that anybody did anything wrong. It just means we need a judge to decide something."

"I don't feel ready to talk about that yet, but I will when I am able."

"You can have a hug anytime you want one."

"I will pick you up next week at 9 A.M. for our visiting time. I know it is important to do exactly what I say I will do."

"You can talk about your feelings if you want to, but I won't pressure you to talk to me."

[Also see: Divorce; Parents Who Fight; Stepparent Families]

MONEY

CHILDREN HAVE a hard time understanding money. The very young child often believes that the more coins the better—five pennies are better than one dime. School-age children may be confused by the use of credit cards since no money is needed and the same card pays for a small toy as well as a television. They may not comprehend that the bill must be paid later.

By the time children enter kindergarten, they begin to understand that money is earned from work, and that some people are rich, others are poor.

What Parents Can Do:

- Children can be given an allowance when they are around four or five years of age. The idea of budgeting can be introduced by telling the child that some of the money must be saved, some must be given to God (tithed), and some can be spent any way the child chooses.

- Some parents consider the age in years of the child as the number of dollars per month a fair allowance. This may be too much money for some families to afford. In addition, the amount given to the child should reflect the expectation of what the child is to buy with the money. Ten dollars a month is too much to spend on candy!

- The child's allowance should not be connected to doing household chores. Chores are expected of every family member simply because they live in the family. Children should be encouraged to earn extra money by doing special jobs, however.

- Children should not be paid for receiving good grades. Studying hard and earning the best grades possible for the child's ability is expected.

- Parents should explain clearly the consequences they attach to the allowance. What will happen, for example, if the child spends all his or her money, has none to buy ice cream, and everyone else is going for a cone.

- When children spend all of their money, parents may choose to loan them money and charge interest. Children will learn that the inability to delay gratification is expensive.

- Older children may spend all their clothing allowance on one dress or pair of jeans and have no money for underwear or shoes. Parents must tell the child what will happen before such a circumstance.

- At the same time, children need permission to make mistakes and suffer the consequences of their decisions. When parents fix a child's financial problems by withholding future allowances, the child cannot learn to solve his money problems. Even a six-year-old child can learn to save for two weeks to buy a special toy.

- Parents can tell their children general information about the family finances, such as the fact that they do not have enough money to buy a car yet but are saving money every month for it.

- Children are frightened when parents are overwhelmed with worry about money. Some children will assume responsibility to try to help in unrealistic ways by lemonade stands or selling toys. Children should be reassured that although this is a hard time, they will have all of their needs met.

Parents Can Teach Children about Money By:

- Explaining the restaurant bill, tax, tip
- Comparing prices on similar products at the store
- Taking children with you to deposit money in savings

- Reading a missionary letter and telling the children how happy you feel to be able to use your tithe money to help missionaries

- Telling children that Jesus talked about money in the Bible; he said that how you spend money shows what is most important to you

Parents can talk to children about advertising techniques designed to make consumers feel they can't live without a certain product. Say that ads try to trick people. Let children choose how they will give their tithe money: put it in the offering at Sunday school, give it to missionaries, or send it to a homeless shelter.

▶ WHAT THE BIBLE SAYS:

Proverbs 11:28   Those who trust in riches will be ruined. But a good person will be as healthy as a green leaf.

Malachi 3:10   "Bring to the storehouse a tenth of what you gain. Then there will be food in my house. Test me in this," says the Lord of heaven's armies. "I will open the windows of heaven for you. I will pour out more blessings than you have room for."

Hebrews 13:5   Keep your lives free from the love of money. And be satisfied with what you have. God has said, "I will never leave you; I will never forget you."

▶ WHAT TO SAY:

"It is hard to wait when you really want to buy something."

"Jesus told a wonderful story in the Bible about how to spend money. Daddy is going to read it, and then we'll talk about how we spend money in this family."

"Here is the record of your savings account. Look how much interest you have earned this past year!"

"I know that it is hard to have no money left and have such a long time to wait before your next allowance. How could you prevent this from happening again?"

"Some people have lots of money, but they don't seem as happy as our family. Money doesn't make people happy."

"You can watch TV when your chores are done. Next week you may choose to get your jobs done in the morning, so you won't miss your favorite program."

"When we put the tithe envelope in the church offering, one of the church leaders will divide the money into the different needs of the church, such as paying the pastor, paying for the water and lights, and giving to the poor."

"Some Christians give much more than their tithe to God. The Bible teaches that God loves a person who gives cheerfully."

[Also see: Gangs; Poverty]

NATURAL
DISASTERS

What Children Might Experience:

FIRES, FLOODS, earthquakes, and hurricanes occur with little warning and can cause deep trauma for the children who experience them. Stress and trauma come from multiple sources. The child's friends may have been hurt or may have died, and pets may be lost or injured. Adults, primary sources of security, may be angry, crying, or emotionally unavailable to the child while they focus on the unfolding events. In addition, familiar routine and schedules are disturbed.

Children cannot differentiate degrees of threat and are unable to sort through potential harm from actual danger. It is difficult for children to get away from the tension due to round-the-clock radio and television coverage that graphically shows death tolls, destruction, and bloody scenes.

Children may remember different parts of the event at different times. It takes a long time for the whole story to emerge. Reminiscing about the disaster will likely occur for years to come for both adults and children.

Initially, children and adults are often stunned, numb, and in shock. Children may be clingy, frightened, and questioning at this stage. In the beginning it just does not seem real. Don't assume that these early responses reflect the feelings that will emerge later. Later feelings include sadness, guilt, anger, anxiety, and stomachaches. It is not uncommon for young children to be afraid to go to school because they fear separation from their parents.

Children respond to difficult times in ways that are consistent with their personalities. Most children will not need professional help if parents provide the support they need by psychological first aid.

What Parents Can Do to Help a Child following a Disaster:

- Invite children to help clean up debris after the disaster. Working will combat feelings of helplessness and allow them to be with adults who are restoring pre-disaster life.

- Children usually play out their feelings and should be given time and permission to play while adults work. Hard physical play is helpful, and toys such as dress-up clothes and dolls that allow the child to act out the disaster are helpful.

- Provide opportunities to express feelings through painting, cutting out pictures from magazines and pasting them in a collage, listening to feeling songs, and encouraging play with clay.

- If a child must be hospitalized, at least one family member should try to remain with him continually.

- Give the child honest answers about the disaster. Don't attempt to reassure the child with statements that are likely to be proved false later. When you don't know the answer, admit it.

- Read stories about children's experiences in a disaster. Children like to know how others felt and responded.

- Most children have difficulty sleeping following a disaster and need some of the comfort methods that were helpful when they were younger, such as night-lights and extra time with the parent at bedtime.

- Hold and comfort the child often.

- Share your anxieties with other adults, not with children.

- Remind children that the family has been through other hard times and can make it through this one.

▶ WHAT THE BIBLE SAYS:

Psalm 55:22   Give your worries to the Lord. He will take care of you. He will never let good people down.

Psalm 57:1   Be merciful to me, God. Be merciful to me because I come to you for protection. I will come to you as a bird comes for protection under its mother's wings until the trouble has passed.

Proverbs 3:24-25   You won't need to be afraid when you lie down. When you lie down, your sleep will be peaceful. You won't need to be afraid of trouble coming suddenly.

▶ WHAT TO SAY:

"This is a scary, hard time, but we'll stay close together as a family."

"Tell me when you need a hug."

"It's not 'being a baby' to need me to stay with you until you fall asleep. You won't always need this."

"What you are feeling is the way any child would feel who had been in a major flood."

"You and your brother will probably have different feelings at different times. He may be frightened when you are mad."

"Your daddy and I are very upset about losing our home, but we can take care of you. We're not mad at you about anything."

"You don't have to act strong and brave. It's okay to cry."

"I don't know why no one in our family was hurt, when our neighbors lost so much. Bad things happen and we don't always know why. God loves them as much as he loves us."

"It's going to take awhile for us to get over this."

"God knows how we are feeling and he is right here with us."

[Also see: Fears and Worries; Why Bad Things Happen to Good People]

PARENTS WHO FIGHT

What Children Might Experience:

CHILDREN ARE frightened by serious arguments between parents, and they may be terrified by fighting that involves hitting or name calling. Children know they are dependent on the protection of their parents, and out-of-control parents cannot offer the security children need to feel safe. On the other hand, children who never observe adults fight and make up are deprived of the opportunity to learn how to resolve differences. Children need to know that it is possible to argue with someone yet still love them. Teach children that anger is a normal emotion so that when they feel angry themselves, they will not feel guilty or overwhelmed.

Trying to hide serious differences between parents is seldom effective. Children sense the tension. If children are deprived of role models of parents who argue, express themselves thoroughly, make compromises, and love each other through it all, they will lack these skills in their own adult relationships.

Even with good modeling, very young children cannot manage their angry feelings without clear direction and limit-setting from parents. The best modeling in the world won't prevent a four-year-old from hitting a child who takes his toy. Most children become angry because they are frustrated. Children who can learn to talk it out instead of act it out will acquire lifelong skills. Teach children to think before they act. Parents are not the only models that children receive about how to handle anger. Children who watch violence on TV may be influenced by these negative models. Parents should limit viewing of violent TV shows, and when violence is witnessed, state, "Hitting someone is *never* a good way to express anger."

What Parents Can Do:

Sometimes children are identified as the problem in a family because it is easier to blame a child than for parents to assume responsibility for their relationship. Children who are blamed for parents' fighting will have difficulty developing a good sense of self-worth. If there is a great deal of fighting in the family, children often feel lonely.

The young child needs to be reassured that even though her parents are mad at each other, no one will be physically hurt. Children can be told that they will have many disagreements as they grow up, but they can learn to talk about these differences. When differences can't be resolved, they may need to walk away from a person who doesn't want to talk through the problem.

Tell children that God cares about how people get along in a family. Children can be told that they don't need to pretend that their parents' fighting doesn't bother them. It helps to tell children that they do not have to solve this problem all by themselves. Offer yourself to help them.

Parents Who Fight Frequently or in Demeaning Ways Can:

- Attend an anger management class
- Schedule regular times to talk about issues privately—don't allow tension to build up
- Look at the source of the anger; are the fights about control? are they the result of abusing alcohol? are they caused by lack of knowing better ways to deal with angry feelings?
- Include hard physical exercise into lifestyle to reduce tension

- See a professional therapist, especially if fights result in any physical or emotional injury to either parent

Teaching Children How to Respond to Violence:

Children learn to respond to aggressive, pushy, angry people by watching the model of their parents. No verbal direction will have as much power as the examples of problem-solving children witness in their family. Teach children the following ways to respond to bullies:

- Walk away from a bully. Do not give him the satisfaction of responding.
- There is nothing shameful about being bullied. Children often feel that if they were not "such a nerd" that a bully wouldn't pick on them.
- Bullies have not learned correct ways of solving problems.
- If they are in physical danger, especially being threatened by someone bigger than they are, they should not fight. They should report the incident as soon as possible to a helpful adult.
- Tell a bully to "STOP," and then walk away with shoulders held high.

▶ WHAT THE BIBLE SAYS:

Colossians 3:8 But now put these things out of your life: anger, bad temper, doing or saying things to hurt others, and using evil words when you talk.

2 Timothy 2:23-24 Stay away from foolish and stupid arguments. You know that such arguments grow into bigger arguments. And a servant of the Lord must not quarrel!

▶ WHAT TO SAY:

"Children are never the cause of adult fighting. We need to choose better ways of dealing with our disagreements."

"I know that it was embarrassing for you last night when we had a loud argument and your friend was here and heard it. Please forgive me. I will try to be more sensitive to your needs."

"It is okay to talk to your school counselor about your feelings. You don't have to keep our family problems a secret. Mom and Dad need help, and you deserve help also."

"You don't have to deal with that bully all by yourself. Your teacher and your dad and I are going to help you."

"You shouldn't try to stop your dad from hitting me. You can call our neighbors and they will help you figure out what to do. If they are not at home, you can call the police and they will come to help."

"Don't talk to your mom about the fighting while she is angry or in the middle of an argument. Wait until she is calm and then tell her that you feel scared and want some help."

"Not every family has hurtful fights, but every family has disagreements and some problems. People can learn to talk about the problems without yelling."

"Let's figure out some ways you could act around that bully."

"When we fight, leave the room and go to a safe place."

"Sometimes parents call their children bad names when they are angry. But just because they say something doesn't mean that it is true. God knows the truth about how precious you are."

"What do you worry about most when we fight?"

"The fact that we are fighting doesn't mean that we are going to get a divorce."

[Also see: Alcoholism; Divorce; Living with a Single Parent; Stepparent Families]

POVERTY

What Children Might Experience:

CHILDREN IN Christian homes may hear strong statements about poor people and become confused when they hear contradictory statements by other Christians. For example, they may be told:

- "People should work for their money, and giving to poor people simply encourages them to expect handouts." Later, the child may hear, "It isn't compassionate to require that poor people listen to a gospel sermon before being fed at a rescue mission. Christians should feed people because it is the right thing to do."

- Or someone may say: "If Christians give money to street people, the money will probably be used to buy drugs or alcohol, so the money is wasted." At Sunday school the child hears: "Whenever we give to others, we are giving to Christ. Good deeds are the natural outgrowth of Christian faith."

- At times a truth is combined with an error and the child does not know what to believe, for example, someone might say: "The Bible teaches that the world will become worse and worse before Christ's second coming, and therefore it's useless to fix social problems."

- Some statements about the poor reflect the bias of the particular family, such as: "One of the differences between fundamental and liberal churches is that liberal churches focus on social concerns such as feeding the poor, but fundamental churches focus on teaching the Bible."

Children are taught about social issues, including homelessness, at school, but for many the first significant experience with poverty occurs during a church mission trip to a third-world country during high school. The contrast of the teen's middle-class affluent lifestyle compared with the evident poverty they observe is blatant. Children may be told in school that the number of Americans who are on a diet is approximately twice the number of Africans who are presently starving. Some children will attend classes with children of migrant workers who live in shacks or homeless children living in shelters. Children may grow up in homes which have always been poor, or they may experience sudden poverty when the primary wage earner loses employment. These situations are stressful in different ways. Children can learn that not everyone who is poor fits in the same category.

What Parents Can Do:

What to Tell Children about Why People Are Poor:

- Some are poor because they have an incurable mental illness or physical disability and are unable to work.
- Some are too old to work.
- Some choose not to work.
- Some can't get a job because they don't have the skills, such as reading.
- Some are poor because they resist the structure of a work setting and a boss who tells them what to do.
- Some people are unable to work because of an addiction to alcohol or drugs.
- Some people lose their jobs because the company closes.
- Some people would rather live on welfare.

Parents Can Demonstrate Acceptance of Poor People By:

- Attending church services in an economically poor neighborhood

- Living in a poor neighborhood and working to improve it
- Volunteering as a family to help at Christian rescue missions
- Donating used clothing and household goods to furnish shelters
- Speaking with respect at home about poor people
- Placing more value on a person's character than how much money a family has
- Maintaining humility about job skills, intelligence, and good parental modeling (Some people have a heritage that others do not have.)

▶ WHAT THE BIBLE SAYS:

Matthew 8:20   Jesus said to him, "The foxes have holes to live in. The birds have nests to live in. But the Son of Man has no place where he can rest his head."

1 John 3:17   Suppose a believer is rich enough to have all that he needs. He sees his brother in Christ who is poor and does not have what he needs. What if the believer does not help the poor brother? Then the believer does not have God's love in his heart.

▶ WHAT TO SAY:

"Christ taught that it isn't enough to give money to help poor people. We are to love them, take care of them, and tell them about Jesus."

"It is wrong to require that only people who become Christians will receive help from Christian agencies. We are to do the right thing, no matter what the other person's choice is about accepting Christ."

"Daddy is bringing some men over to help him on the farm today. They need the money, and Daddy knows it is best for them to earn money, not just receive a handout."

"Sometimes people, such as the mentally ill, cannot earn enough to pay for medical care and food and clothes. Other people have not been taught how to keep a job, but they can learn."

"I know that it is hard to pass by these people who are begging on the street, but it isn't smart to give them money directly since we don't

know how they will spend it. We will give to a rescue mission or the Salvation Army and let these organizations use it to help the poor."

"We're not better simply because we have a nice house, health insurance, and good clothes. These are gifts from God. Everything we have belongs to God."

"You inherited a good mind, have parents who have shown you how to work hard to earn money, and you live in a rich country. These are all gifts that some others do not have."

"Let's sort through the clothes that you have outgrown and take them to the homeless shelter."

"Many children in the United States go to bed hungry and don't have adequate health care."

[Also see: Gangs; Money]

PREJUDICE

BY THE time children are five years old they begin to discover what others feel about racial heritage and religion through watching television programs that contain ethnic jokes or through stories about people of their race or affiliation. Children also note how they are treated by peers and adults, and they compare that with how other children are treated. Children with low self-esteem are more likely to be prejudiced than children who feel good about themselves.

What Children Might Experience:

Parents of minority children may place extraordinary pressure on their children to succeed socially or academically in an attempt to contradict stereotypical attitudes. Many children who belong to minority groups will have many friends from the majority culture. However, these children will usually retain a sense of being different. Although they are taught at school that diversity is culturally enriching and that we have much to gain by honoring each race, children may nevertheless feel the subtle rejection often present among peers.

In some schools, black children are more likely to be blamed for wrongdoing by peers and adults than white children in the same classroom. These prejudicial acts create an early sense of injustice, discouragement, and shame. As self-esteem becomes damaged, children have less ability to succeed academically and to maximize other skills.

What Parents Can Do to Combat Prejudice:

- Tell your child why prejudicial remarks hurt the feelings of other children.

- Clearly state that talk which puts others down is not allowed and will have consequences. (An appropriate consequence for a school-age child might be to write a paper about an outstanding person from the minority race.)

- Read stories that show successful children and people of all races.

- Invite families of other races and cultures to spend holidays with your family. Share their customs.

- Talk in positive ways about your own respect for others who are different from your family.

- Trace your family tree so that your children understand that all of us came from other countries and that their great-great-grandparents may have spoken another language.

- Tell children it is no more acceptable to use others to gain what the child wants than it is to demean others. For example, being especially nice to a rich child in order to swim in their pool is also wrong.

- Teach children that prejudice may include negative feelings about children who are overweight, slow learners, or poor. Prejudice may also include excluding girls from sports teams.

- Encourage your child to speak up against prejudice.

- Take advantage of television news or newspaper articles to talk about prejudice and how Christians are to respond to it.

- Tell children that God made all races and that one race is not better than another. Since Jesus was born in the Middle East, he probably had dark skin and he was born in a Jewish family.

- Help children be sensitive about nicknames, names of pets, or names of clubs so that no racially offensive words are used. For example, many major sports teams have names that refer to Native Americans, such as Redskins, Indians, or Braves. These names might be hurtful to others. When children have the opportunity to choose names, help them select names that allow everyone to feel good.

▶ WHAT THE BIBLE SAYS:

1 Thessalonians 5:15 Be sure that no one pays back wrong for wrong. But always try to do what is good for each other and for all people.

James 2:1 So never think that some people are more important than others.

▶ WHAT TO SAY:

"Our way of doing things isn't necessarily the best way. There are lots of good ways to celebrate Christmas."

"There are outstanding leaders from every race."

"We're more alike than we are different."

"Learning about the customs and music and food of people from China shows respect. Our Chinese friends would be pleased that we want to understand."

"That is an unkind slang expression about people of another race. It is not a word that our family uses. The correct word is ..."

"Some children are prejudiced because they have not been taught that it is wrong."

"The fact that she has a hard time learning doesn't mean that all children from that race are slow learners, and the fact that he is a good dancer doesn't mean that all children from that race dance well."

"Would you like to work on a project with Lamont at our house after school?"

"One of the reasons I think this day camp will be a fun experience for you is that you will get to make friends with children from other races, and they will get to play with you."

"How do you think she felt when Joe said that about her family?"

[Also see: AIDS; Overweight; Physical Disabilities]

ROCK MUSIC

What Parents Need to Know:

CHRISTIAN PARENTS and teenagers will likely have heated discussions about music. The average teenager listens to rock music five hours a day. Christian teenagers may defend listening to rap, grunge, or heavy metal rock music with a variety of reasons, but to most parents this music represents rebellion, permissive sexual attitudes, tolerance or encouragement of drug use, defiance against authority, or hopelessness. In many states underage children may legally purchase obscene recordings.

Adults view rock concerts as sites of deafening noise and swaying, mesmerized teenagers being led by half-naked, long-haired school dropouts. Even Christian music seems to be without socially redeeming value to many Christian parents. Teens may accuse adults of rejecting their music based purely on personal taste, not because there is anything wrong with it. Teens like what they know. Children who have little exposure to symphonies, choral groups, opera, or other quality music while growing up are unlikely to choose it as teenagers.

Music may be one of the most prominent stress releasers used by adolescents. Listening to music provides freedom from thinking about the demands and problems of their lives. The despair commonly expressed in music speaks for the feelings of many frustrated teenagers.

What Parents Can Do:

- Young children should not listen to heavy metal, rap, or grunge music. The subject matter of this music is not appropriate for children under ten years old.

- Separate style of music from content. It is no more appropriate for adults to listen to mellow music that advocates sexual infidelity than for youth music that condones it.

- Behavior which is totally forbidden becomes more attractive than behavior which has limits.

- Show interest in music selections, listen carefully to the words of each song, ask questions about the recording artists, and seek an explanation about why the teenager particularly likes a recording. This provides accountability without condemning.

- Give teenagers guidelines for music that is acceptable. Allow music that:
  1. Has lyrics that encourage good behavior and attitudes.
  2. Makes the listener love God and respect others (such as those in authority and women) more.
  3. Provides a good model by the musicians' lifestyle.
  4. Expresses values that are consistent with what the Bible teaches.
  5. Sets a good example for others.

- Avoid nagging, badgering, threatening. Ask God for wisdom. Pray for the teenagers' listening habits.

- Consider other forms of musical groups' influence, such as posters in the child's room and music magazines. Offer to replace these with acceptable substitutes at your expense; in other words, trade them in. This can also be done with inappropriate CDs and tapes, which can be exchanged for better music.

- Provide fun family experiences which do not include listening to music such as going out for pizza or playing softball.

- Forbid attendance at heavy metal rock concerts. Again, provide an alternative on the night of the concert, such as a trip out of town with the family and an invitation for the child to bring a friend.

▶ WHAT THE BIBLE SAYS:

Psalm 150 Praise the Lord! Praise God in his Temple. Praise him in his mighty heaven. Praise him for his strength. Praise him for his greatness. Praise him with trumpet blasts. Praise him with harps and lyres. Praise him with tambourines and dancing. Praise him with stringed instruments and flutes. Praise him with loud cymbals. Praise him with crashing cymbals. Let everything that breathes praise the Lord. Praise the Lord!

▶ WHAT TO SAY:

"I know that you believe you aren't really influenced by the words of those songs. I see your attitudes changing though, and it concerns me."

"You are probably right, those musicians aren't satanists. But do you respect their pretending that they are, just so they can sell CDs?"

"You can listen to your Christian music tapes one hour a day if your homework is done."

"Would you like to learn to play the guitar or piano? Your dad and I will provide lessons if you are interested."

"I bought four tickets to your favorite Christian music group. You can take whoever you choose. I'll drive."

"If you were the parent, what rules would you have for your children about watching MTV?"

"Let's talk about this TV program after it's over."

"I'm praying that you will have the courage to change the radio station when songs are played that don't honor God."

"I'd like you to write down the words on that tape, and let's talk about them."

"What do you think the people who are in that heavy metal group will be doing in ten years?"

"I really respect your good judgment in the music you bought today."

[Also see: Television, Videos, and Movies]

STEPPARENT FAMILIES

AS OF the mid-1990s, families in the United States have more stepchildren than nonstepchildren. Life in a stepparent family is full of potential land mines for the unsuspecting parent and child. The parent, full of newlywed love and seeing the world through rose-colored glasses, may assume whatever is good for the parent will be joyfully accepted by the child. Beginning life in a stepparent home is rarely that uncomplicated!

Children can learn that God will help them through the adjustments of living in a stepparent family. Young children and children who have been given plenty of time to build a relationship with the new stepparent may come to see the new family as a good thing. A new stepfather may provide additional, focused attention. Boys in particular will often improve in school performance and maturity if they have a loving relationship with a stepfather.

What Children Might Experience:

Even so, children will feel highly stressed in spite of the happiness of the parents. There are many reasons this may happen, including:

- Children who had their biological parent all to themselves may resent sharing their parent with the new spouse and with stepsiblings.

- Children who have been treated as their parent's confidant prior to the marriage may not enjoy being relegated to the role of child again.
- The child's position in the birth order of the family will likely change. An oldest child may suddenly find himself as the youngest in the new family.
- Divorced fathers who have been denied contact with their biological children may resist emotional ties to the new stepchildren out of guilt.

Stepparents rarely have the privacy and intimacy they imagined. Instead of romantic dinners, they have miniature golf. Tension may build. Quarreling in the new family is stressful to children who assume this fighting is a prelude to another divorce. Unfortunately, in fact, 60 percent of these remarriages will end in divorce.

What Parents Can Do:

Discipline in the stepfamily can be difficult. For the first few years it works best for the biological parent to discipline whenever possible. When this isn't possible, it helps to have the biological parent tell the child that he is asking the stepparent to act for him while he is gone.

It will help for the stepparent to say that she does not want to replace the noncustodial parent. Say, "I am not your biological parent, but I am acting as your mother now." Expect rejection initially! Unity cannot be forced.

Initially there may be more fighting in the stepparent home due to the many changes and adjustments. Rules and discipline are often different at the stepparent and biological homes; behavior that is acceptable at one home will get the children in trouble at the other home. Children can learn the two sets of rules, but it will take time.

Children may feel jealous and resentful of their new stepsiblings. It helps if each parent spends time alone with each child. Children may lose contact with grandparents, so arrange these visits for continuity.

▶ WHAT THE BIBLE SAYS:

1 Thessalonians 2:7-8   We were like a mother caring for her little children. Because we loved you, we were happy to share God's Good News with you. But not only that, we were also happy to share even our own lives with you.

1 Peter 2:13   Obey the people who have authority in this world. Do this for the Lord.

▶ WHAT TO SAY:

"Your dad and I are different people and like to do different kinds of things with you. I think you can enjoy being with both of us."

"It is hard to know what to do when you have two tickets to the school play. You can take turns inviting your dad and me one time, and your mom and her husband another time."

"We will have family night every week and talk about ways to make our new family a great place to live."

"You don't have to call me Mom. You already have a mom. You can call me Kathy."

"I know that you have mixed feelings now. I think I would, too, if I were a kid in a new stepfamily."

"The bedrooms will be rotated every six months so that no one has the biggest room all the time."

"You can tell us what you choose after your home visits, but we won't pry. We will be glad if you had a good time, and we won't think badly of your mom if you had a hard time."

"Getting used to a stepparent family takes a long time for most kids. We don't expect you to like everything right away."

"You don't have to take sides between your mom and dad. I know that you love them both."

[Also see: Divorce; Living with a Single Parent; Parents Who Fight]

TELEVISION, VIDEOS, AND MOVIES

What Parents Need to Know:

CHILDREN WILL be exposed to a variety of opinions among Christian families about watching TV. The average Christian child will watch twenty-two hours of TV every week and witness thousands of murders on TV before leaving high school. Children spend more time watching TV than going to school, going to church, in one-on-one time with their parents, or in playing with friends. Some families avoid attending movies in theaters but rent similar films to watch at home on the VCR. Other families severely limit the amount of time children spend watching TV, even good programming, because they believe it is better for children to live life than to watch it.

Violence

Many families object to sexual programming but not to violence on TV. Others tolerate violence in cartoons but not in other programs. There is a known correlation between watching violence on TV and aggressive behavior in children. The more TV violence the child views before the third grade, the more aggressive the child's behavior will be for the next ten years. Some psychologists believe that watching violence only accentuates an already present tendency to be aggressive, rather than causing violent behavior. They point to the fact that children have been listening to violent fairy tales and Bible stories for years without any harm. The tendency to be aggressive is more likely to come from experiencing violence at home.

Children can become frightened or worried about being safe from watching violent TV programs. Parents who have strong feelings about what their children watch on TV will need to communicate their requirements to families of playmates and to baby-sitters. Young adolescents are frequently allowed to rent PG- or R-rated videos from stores without parental consent.

What Parents Can Do:

How to Decide What to Avoid Watching on TV:

- Does the program, whether on TV, video, or movie please Christ in thoughts, words, and actions? If a film does not do this, it is wrong to watch it.
- Does the film give a biblical view of women? Does it show sex without respect for women? Is brutal sex portrayed as normal?
- Does the film contain frequent profanity?
- Does the film present stories about people getting away with sin? Or are the effects of sin shown?
- Does the film communicate truth or lies about God?
- Does the film make you want to obey God more?
- Does the film teach biblical ways of solving problems with others? Or teach that it is okay to beat somebody up?
- Is the film frightening, disrespectful, or a poor example to others?
- Does the amount of time spent watching TV cause the child to avoid facing the real world, doing chores, finishing homework, or making friends?

Parents should watch at least one episode of a program before allowing children to watch. When considering TV viewing, think about the impact of commercials. If the advertisers have done their job well, commercials encourage the child to want things that are not good for them, such as junk food or the latest toy. Writers of commercials know how to appeal to children. The intent of a commercial is to make money for the manufacturer, not to help children. TV and videos should not be used as a baby-sitting device.

Some Television Programs and Videos Are Helpful to Watch:

- Game shows based on knowledge can be fun, entertaining, and educational.
- Programs that present options for solving problems can stimulate.
- Television offers a needed way to relax and laugh.
- TV news promotes understanding of complex problems with information about the world with maps, and by presenting two sides of an issue.

▶ WHAT THE BIBLE SAYS:

Psalm 119:37 Keep me from looking at worthless things. Let me live by your word.

Matthew 6:22-23 The eye is a light for the body. If your eyes are good, then your whole body will be full of light. But if your eyes are evil, then your whole body will be full of darkness. And if the only light you have is really darkness, then you have the worst darkness.

▶ WHAT TO SAY:

"You can watch TV when your homework is done, but the TV cannot be turned on until your work is completed."

"Christians are to think about things that are pure and wholesome. That's why our family doesn't go to R-rated movies."

"That movie implies that is okay to have sex before you are married. That's not what God's Word says."

"Hearing bad language on TV can make it easier to use those words."

"Someday you will be able to turn the TV off when a program is not helpful for you. In the meantime, I will do it for you."

"Let's all watch that program together and talk about it afterwards."

"You've watched TV for an hour. Now it is time to go outside and play."

"I know that you hear those same bad words at school, but we don't allow them to be used in our home, even on TV."

"What they are doing on TV is pretend and nobody really got hurt. But if that actually happened, it would hurt someone very badly."

"On Sunday we will look through the TV guide and circle the programs you are permitted to watch this week."

"You may watch one hour of approved TV in a day, or you can save the time for two hours on one day."

"Don't sit any closer than this line when you watch TV. It is bad for your eyes."

[Also see: Rock Music]

WAR

What Children Need to Know:

PRESCHOOLERS PLAY with war toys, and by the time children are six or seven years old, they begin to understand war and peace between countries. However, throughout childhood children know more about war than peacemaking. They have little understanding about how countries solve problems other than through fighting.

Young children generalize information. When their country is at war, children believe that all people from the other country are cruel, aggressive, and bad, and that everyone from their own country is kind, loving, and good. Neither is true.

Christians disagree about how conflict between countries should be resolved. Some Christians believe it is wrong to go to war because we are commanded to love our enemies and pray for those who persecute us. One of the Ten Commandments states, "Thou shalt not kill." Others believe it is not our job to punish people. God will take care of people who do wrong.

Other Christians believe it is right to go to war because God uses Christians to stop evil in the world through "just wars." The Bible says we are to obey our government leaders, and in the Old Testament, God often ordered his people to destroy their enemies.

How Parents Can Support Children:

• Children may have difficulty understanding why God allows

war to happen. They can be told that God's plan was that people would get along with each other, but that God gives people the freedom to choose, and sometimes they make wrong choices.

- Children feel the tension of the adults in their home. TV reports of conflict and the numbers who have died cause anxiety in adults. Children know their parents are worried. Adults should not deny their feelings but teach children what to do when they feel frightened. They can be taught to pray, talk about how they feel, and focus on our security in God.

- Children have no way of assessing the amount of danger they are in. "Could a scud missile hit our house?" Take children's questions seriously and give them factual information: "We are in no danger because a scud couldn't reach our house."

- During war, parents may spend excessive time watching TV war reports, and children lose the balance of conversation about fun, light subjects, and silly play. Children are helped by hugs, one-on-one time with the parent in nonwar related talks, and hard physical play.

- Children's deep fears are minimized by simplistic reassurances, such as "don't worry." These statements increase children's fears because they feel no one understands. Parents can read stories of people in the Bible who were afraid and were comforted and helped by God.

- Preschoolers are frightened by too much information about war. They simply want to know that their parents will take care of them.

- Children who hear constant criticism of their country's political leaders have higher anxiety about being safe. Praying for leaders even when parents disagree with them helps children.

- Children need to understand the impact of war on a country, such as that homes are destroyed, children are hurt, and many innocent people die, not just who is winning.

- Families who host foreign students provide children the opportunity to develop friendships with people from other countries.

- Parents should avoid telling children that God will keep our country from war, since children may wonder why Christians in other countries are dying in wars.

▶ WHAT THE BIBLE SAYS:

Matthew 24:6 You will hear about wars and stories of wars that are coming. But don't be afraid. These things must happen before the end comes.

James 4:1 Do you know where your fights and arguments come from? They come from the selfish desires that make war inside you.

1 Peter 3:8-9 Finally, all of you should live together in peace. Try to understand each other. Love each other as brothers. Be kind and humble. Do not do wrong to a person to pay him back for doing wrong to you. Or do not insult someone to pay him back for insulting you. But ask God to bless that person. Do this, because you yourselves were called to receive a blessing.

▶ WHAT TO SAY:

"Your mom and I don't let angry people determine how we are going to act. The fact that they are angry doesn't mean that we need to respond with anger."

"We feel sad and worried about the war in the Middle East. There are many people suffering in those countries."

"When you hear about the war, what do you wonder about?"

"You were really patient with your little sister while I was on the phone. Thank you for being a peacemaker."

"Some Christians believe it is wrong to go to war, and we respect these differences."

"Jesus showed us how to solve differences without fighting."

"There are missionaries in both of the countries at war as well as Christian families on both sides."

"War is especially hard for children because their daddies often must leave home to fight in the war. Some of them will die."

"Let's pray that the war will stop."

Medical
Topics

AIDS
(Acquired Immune Deficiency Syndrome)

IDS STANDS for:

Acquired—not born with

Immune—body's defense system

Deficiency—not working properly

Syndrome—a group of signs and symptoms

AIDS is caused by a virus called HIV (human immune virus). If the virus gets into the bloodstream, it attacks certain parts of the body's immune system. Some illnesses that the body normally fights off become problems.

Parents can model loving attitudes by serving families who have a person with AIDS. Children can help by coloring pictures for the family, or by helping with cooking food to deliver to them. A child who has had firsthand experience with a person with AIDS will have a different attitude about the disease than the child with no contact with the disease.

What Children Need to Know:

- Tell the truth, no matter what the child asks. The simplest, correct answer is usually the best one. Then invite the child to ask the next question.

- Children may wonder why people do things that are dangerous and could give them the HIV virus. You can say that:
  1. Sometimes people don't know that it is an unsafe activity (for example, touching someone's blood without gloves).
  2. Sometimes they may think that the virus won't get into them even if they are doing something unsafe.

- Children will observe the parent's attitude toward persons with AIDS, and that will be more important than the information about AIDS that the parent provides.

- Children hear more than is intentionally taught, and they have built-in lie detectors when they are deceived.

- Tell children that there is no way to tell by looking at someone whether they have the AIDS virus or not. They should practice health safety rules with everyone.

- It is helpful to give children choices about whether they want to visit a person with AIDS or would prefer to stay home with a baby-sitter.

- Children can be told that there is no such thing as safe sex, except in a lifelong marriage that begins with two virgins. They should know that "safer" sex is still dangerous and may not protect them from exposure to the AIDS virus.

- A wise parent will provide some role-playing experiences to give a child practice saying No when invited to do something that is not safe or not moral.

- Children should be told that loving and helping persons with AIDS does not mean that we approve of the choices the person has made.

What Children Might Experience:

- Children feel confused by blaming and condemnation of a loved family member who has HIV disease.

- When the parent is not afraid to be involved in caring, the child will not be afraid.

- A parent with AIDS may be divorced from the custodial parent. These children will already be grieving the loss of the parent through divorce, and now in addition they must grieve the loss of the parent through this life-threatening illness.

- Grief in children may be delayed many years. Not all the feelings about the loved one's death will be apparent initially.

- Grandparents, who are often a source of comfort to children, may be preoccupied with their own grief when the parent of a child has AIDS. They may be unable to support their grandchildren.

- Children will likely receive mandatory school curriculum information about AIDS, but facing the fear, confusion, and sadness of knowing an adult with AIDS is another matter.

▶ WHAT THE BIBLE SAYS:

Galatians 5:13   Serve each other with love.

Ephesians 5:3   But there must be no sexual sin among you. There must not be any kind of evil or greed. Those things are not right for God's holy people.

1 Thessalonians 4:3-5   God wants you to be holy and to stay away from sexual sins. He wants each one of you to learn how to take a wife in a way that is holy and honorable. Don't use your body for sexual sin. The people who do not know God use their bodies for that.

▶ WHAT TO SAY:

"AIDS is a disease that destroys the body's ability to fight other diseases."

"AIDS isn't easy to catch, like a cold. The virus doesn't live outside the body. It only lives in blood and other body fluids."

"A person gets AIDS by contact with the body fluids or blood of a person with the virus, or by being born to a mom who has the virus."

"The AIDS virus can't jump off one surface on to a person. You can choose behavior that controls whether you will be exposed to the virus."

"You can't get AIDS by donating blood to someone."

"When someone asks you to do something that is not safe, say, 'No way, I'm not stupid, and I hope you won't be either.'"

"I don't know the answer to that question, but I will try to find out. I'm glad that you asked."

"Uncle Bob got the virus from another person who has the virus in his blood."

"God didn't make Uncle Bob get AIDS. He got it by being exposed to the virus."

"What do you think it means that a person is 'gay'?"

"Our family believes that sex before marriage is wrong, and that sex is a gift from God only allowed between a husband and wife."

[Also see: Chronic Illness; Homosexuality; Prejudice]

CHRONIC ILLNESS

THE CHILD with a chronic illness, such as diabetes or asthma, will have difficult experiences that other children avoid, such as regular medications or treatments, frequent doctor visits, and occasional hospitalizations during crises.

What the Parent of a Chronically Ill Child Can Do:

- Recognize that a child's illness places enormous stress on a family and marriage. Arrange care for the children so you can be alone with your mate regularly.

- Other children in the family need to feel special. Invite adult relatives to attend soccer games or help with birthday parties so all the children receive focused attention frequently.

- When there are difficult decisions to make, talk with those who give their opinion only when it is sought, allowing you to think out loud without judgment.

- Teach others to do home treatments, so that you feel comfortable being away from home.

- Feeling angry at medical staff is common, and many parents are afraid to express these feelings for fear their child's medical care will be affected. Find a safe place to talk about these feelings.

- Remember that friends and relatives may be initially supportive when the child's illness is diagnosed, but often disappear as the disease becomes chronic. A support group of parents of children with this illness is helpful.

- Pray for the doctor, schoolteacher, the child's friends, and all others involved with your child.
- Start a journal of events when the child is diagnosed. The child will likely see many different medical providers and the information may prove useful.

The crises that occur for chronically ill children are often emergencies accompanied by fear and the potential for disastrous outcomes. A constant state of being on alert may affect children and parents during noncrisis times.

Stress Reduction Techniques for Chronically Ill Children:

Children with chronic illness frequently have invasive, painful tests and injections. Children need to be taught stress reduction methods. Parents can instruct them to:

- Concentrate intently on something else during the painful treatment.
- Say to yourself, "I can handle this."
- Squeeze the hand of an adult or hold tightly to a toy.
- Express feelings about the treatment either verbally or in play or art.
- Take a deep breath and slowly release the air if this is physically possible.

Parents can help by doing the following:

- Hold and comfort the child after the treatment. Praise children for cooperation.
- Provide choices: "Would you like to close your eyes or watch?" "Would you like a blue Band-Aid or a green one?" "Would you like me to help by holding you still, or can you do it on your own?"
- Give information about painful treatments honestly, which will also help reduce stress in children: "Yes, it will hurt." Compare the hurt to some known feeling, "It will feel like a bee sting."

- Tell children about a painful treatment just prior to the time it will occur.

Children with chronic illnesses can develop a sense of competence and self-worth by assuming the role of teacher for other children at school. Writing reports about diabetes or giving talks about the disease allows her to be an authority in a helpful way. Children need practical assistance in managing troublesome events. If a diabetic child attends a birthday party where sweets will be served, for example, parents can offer to send an acceptable dessert substitute.

If the Parent Has a Chronic Illness:

When one of the parents has a chronic, serious illness, family life may revolve around the sick parent. A chronically ill parent may not be able to consistently attend school functions; the child's friends may be restricted from coming over to play at times so that the parent won't be disturbed; and the child may be given additional responsibilities and lose independence. All of these factors will have an impact on childhood. When a parent is chronically ill, children can be given permission to play and enjoy life, and they should be protected from responsibility beyond their years.

▶ WHAT THE BIBLE SAYS:

Isaiah 40:29-31   The Lord gives strength to those who are tired. He gives more power to those who are weak. Even boys become tired and need to rest. Even young men trip and fall. But the people who trust the Lord will become strong again. They will be able to rise up as an eagle in the sky. They will run without needing rest. They will walk without becoming tired.

▶ WHAT TO SAY:

"I don't blame you for being tired of giving yourself shots."

"What have you learned about diabetes that you think other kids should know?"

"If you are matter-of-fact when you talk to other kids about your treatments, I think they will accept it."

"Are you feeling worried? Tell me about it."

"I like the way you take good care of your equipment. It shows how responsible you are."

"I may not know all the answers about your disease, but I will try to find out, so please ask anytime you wonder about something."

"I know that you don't like feeling different. Let's figure out a way to minimize the differences and focus on the ways you are alike."

"I'm so glad that you can laugh about some of the problems."

"How you feel physically affects how you feel about your friends, yourself, and your relationship to God."

"God understands when you are angry about being sick. Being angry is a normal feeling."

"I have heard about a support group for children who have asthma. Would you like to try it out?"

"Here is a book about a child with diabetes. How is your experience different? How is it the same?"

[Also see: AIDS; Dementia; Going to the Hospital; Organ Transplants]

CRITICAL ILLNESS

NOTHING IS more frightening for family and friends than the critical illness of a young child. Coping methods that have been helpful in previous experiences may not be adequate to deal with the stress of the catastrophic illness of a child. Initially, parents may deny the seriousness of the child's illness as a way to survive intolerable stress. In fact, children over six years old are often far ahead of their families in dealing with the potential of death as a result of illness.

What Critically Ill Children Might Experience:

Children younger than five may be more frightened by the separation from their parents than by the nature of the disease. Older children are more likely to understand the possibility of dying from the illness.

Children sense the terrible stress their parents feel and know that something serious is wrong. The phony attempts by parents and other adults to keep cheerful for the child's sake are to no avail. Children have better antennae than adults; they know they have no ordinary illness. In addition to the fear that they might die, children fear separation from their parents and wonder how to cope. Critically ill children worry about how they are supposed to behave in the strange environment of the ICU (Intensive Care Unit). They feel threatened to have so little control and choice about what happens to them in the strange environment of the hospital. Children soon learn that if they are unable to hold still for shots that they will be held down by adults.

What Parents Can Do:

The fears of children change as the illness progresses. It becomes more specific as they learn to fear particular treatments, tests, and examinations, including bone marrow tests and IVs. The longer the young child stays in the hospital, the more traumatic the experience becomes. When it is medically appropriate, very ill young children should receive care at home where they will feel more secure. Many parents learn to give care in the home with the support of visiting medical teams.

Children need to know the name of their illness and the expected course of treatment. Provide as much detail as the child requests. Young children believe that pain is controlled by grownups. Until they realize that adults do not control everything, they fear that they are being punished for the wrong things they have done in the past. They need to be reassured again and again that nothing they have done brought this disease.

Initially, children may cry when their parents leave them at the hospital to go home. Following this, many children become quiet, listless, and depressed as they feel abandoned by their parents. Finally, children may detach emotionally from their parents so that when the parents come to visit, the child ignores them with the attitude of "who needs you, anyway?" Parents need to know that this behavior simply represents emotional survival for the child.

Critically ill children may witness the death of other children and adults in the ICU or pediatric unit. Do not deny the reality of these deaths. Say, "Yes, she died this morning. She was so sick that the medicine wouldn't work anymore."

Frequent contact of the adult with a very ill child is helpful. When a personal visit isn't possible, cards and phone calls convey support and comfort to the child.

The amount of anxiety a child experiences with a critical illness may have to do with the part of his body that is affected: disorders of the heart, genitals, eyes, brain are especially frightening. Be reassuring but don't downplay the child's anxiety.

When the Parent Has a Critical Illness:

Children feel the tension at home when a parent is critically ill even when they have not been given information about the illness. Tell children the name of the illness and what you expect will happen in the immediate future. Avoid long range projections.

Children are sometimes shut out emotionally by the non ill parent who is overwhelmed by the frightening circumstances. Take extra care and time for hugging children; giving them brief, simple updates; reassuring them that neither the child nor the non ill parent is in danger of getting the same sickness; and asking adults known and loved by the child to spend extra time with the child during the crisis.

If the sick parent has been diagnosed with cancer, the child can be told: "Daddy has a disease called cancer, which means that bad cells are growing inside his body. The doctor will perform an operation to take out the bad growth. We expect that Daddy will have to take some strong medicine after the operation to prevent the bad cells from growing again." Don't say that the cancer is a seed that grew and grew. Children generalize and think that such things as tomato seeds or peach pits cause cancer. Reading stories about other children who have a parent with cancer or another critical illness provides information and support. Inviting children to ask questions lets them know there are no scary secrets.

▶ WHAT THE BIBLE SAYS:

2 Thessalonians 2:16-17 We pray that the Lord Jesus Christ himself and God our Father will comfort you and strengthen you in every good thing you do and say. God loved us. Through his grace he gave us a good hope and comfort that continues forever.

James 5:14 If one of you is sick, he should call the church's elders. The elders should pour oil on him in the name of the Lord and pray for him.

▶ WHAT TO SAY:

"Many other children have had this disease. The doctor was able to help them and I think she can help you too."

"I know that it is scary for you when I need to go home. I am leaving

my picture for you to hold. Remember that I am praying for you and loving you while I am at home."

"The X-ray machine is like a giant camera that takes a picture of your insides. It will help the doctor know how to help you. Let's ask if you can see the picture after it is done."

"I'm glad that you told me you are afraid you might die. I worry about that sometimes too. Let's ask God to help us feel calm. The doctor said he thinks you will get well."

"I know that you can't talk. You can squeeze my hand real hard when something hurts."

"You have a blood disease called leukemia. This means you have some bad cells in your blood. The doctor wants you to take some special medicine called chemotherapy to fight the bad cells."

"I will tell you before you have any treatments and what exactly will happen. You have a right to know. There won't be any surprises."

"I'm going to read a story to you about another boy who had cancer and how the doctor helped him get well."

"You can help Mommy while she is so sick by coloring pictures for her room, and by giving her cold drinks. You are an important helper."

"What do you wonder about?"

[Also see: Death of a Parent; Going to the Hospital]

DEMENTIA

CHILDREN WHO live in a family that is affected by someone with Alzheimer's disease or another degenerative brain disease will experience increasing stress in the family. Since these illnesses are often difficult to diagnose, children usually do not know why the family member is acting strangely.

As the disease progresses, the needs of the person with Alzheimer's disease increases and children may receive less parenting as there is less time for them. Be honest with children about the disease. People with Alzheimer's disease don't get better. They will eventually die from the illness. No one knows exactly when that will happen, but usually it takes about ten years.

What Children Might Experience:

Children who have had a loving, close relationship with a grandparent with Alzheimer's disease will feel:

- Sad, as they mourn the loss of this special friendship.
- Confused, when they see the grandparent behave like a child.
- Worried, that the grandparent will be hurt or die.
- Embarrassed, when the grandparent acts inappropriately in front of the child's friends, such as by undressing.
- Hurt, because of the angry lashing out that the grandparent may give the child.
- Resentful, of the time their parents must spend in taking care of the grandparent instead of, for example, going to soccer

games with the child, and resentful of the increased responsibility expected of the child in the home.

Often, the unpredictable behavior of the demented family member will spoil a child's birthday party or other family celebrations.

The person with Alzheimer's disease may wander about the house at night and the child's parents may become increasingly tired and irritable from lack of sleep. Meal times may be unpleasant for the child due to the tension created by the demented person. If the grandparent is sent to a care facility, the parent may feel guilty and the stress will continue at home.

What Parents Can Tell Children:

- The exact name of the illness and the behavior that is caused by the illness, such as forgetting the child's name.
- Nothing they have done caused the illness to happen. It is no one's fault.
- No one knows exactly why some people get Alzheimer's disease. Since most people don't have it when they get older, the child probably won't have it either.
- How to help the grandparent, such as by watching her grandparent when she is in the kitchen so that she does not eat or drink something harmful or hurt herself. Children can have specific assignments in helping to care for the grandparent. These jobs might include:
  1. Taking the grandparent for a walk in the enclosed backyard.
  2. Singing, dancing, or playing music for the grandparent.
  3. Assisting with brushing the grandparent's teeth, giving him fresh fruit, or coloring special pictures for his grandparent's bedroom wall.
  4. Turning the pages on the daily calendar and telling Grandmother the day and month and year.
  5. Returning the grandparent's possessions to the same place every time they are moved.
  6. Thanking children for their kindness, love, and hugs and

saying they are very important to the grandparent and noticed by God.

Parents Can Help By:

- Encouraging children to share the knowledge they have about Alzheimer's disease with other children. They can write papers or give talks about the disorder at school.

- Allowing children to choose how much they want to be involved in the care of the grandparent with Alzheimer's disease. Some children may resent the demands placed on them.

- Valuing and thanking children for their help.

- Reading children's stories about dementia. This helps children know there are other families who live with the same situation.

▶ WHAT THE BIBLE SAYS:

Leviticus 19:32   Show respect to old people. Stand up when they come into the room. Show respect also to your God. I am the Lord.

Isaiah 26:3-4   You, Lord, give true peace. You give peace to those who depend on you. You give peace to those who trust you. So, trust the Lord always.

1 Thessalonians 5:14   Encourage the people who are afraid. Help those who are weak. Be patient with every person.

▶ WHAT TO SAY:

"We are going to have a family meeting to talk about how we can work together to help Grandpa."

"I have been watching the way you are helping Grandma. I think you make God smile."

"Nobody knows exactly what this disease will do. Grandpa might be just the same as he is now for three or four years."

"You deserve time to play and be away from the stress of Grandpa's illness. You don't have to feel bad about that."

"When your friends come over to our house, you can tell them that Grandma has a brain disease that confuses her."

"People are not special because of what they can do or not do. God loves us all just the same."

"Grandpa cries because he is sad about the disease too."

[Also see: Mental Illness]

EATING DISORDERS

What Parents Should Know About:

Anorexia

ANOREXIA IS self-imposed starvation. It is not a loss of appetite but a deliberate control of eating. Fifty percent of girls will diet sometime during their teenage years. One out of ten females twelve and older have struggled with anorexia or bulimia. Girls in junior high school often have strong needs for acceptance based on how they look and are particularly vulnerable to trying to develop the Barbie-doll image. But that is an impossible and unrealistic goal. Sixty percent of models and ballerinas have eating disorders.

Eating disorders occur most often in white, middle- or upper-class girls who fear not being in control. These girls may feel overly praised by their parents for being such good girls. The child's view may be, "since I am given much, much is expected of me." Girls believe that if they are skinny and in need of protection, they will maintain the continued love and care of their parents. Anorexic girls are usually loving, devoted to their families, and well-behaved. They are often model children striving for perfection.

Since families of girls with anorexia may be overly involved in the child's life, independence is difficult for the child. The parents' needs are the most important to the girl and she does not learn to value her own needs, nor even to know the difference between her needs and her parents' needs. One way she can obtain a sense of control, identity, and independence is to starve herself.

Children who become anorexic are often excessively involved in preparing, cooking, and talking about food. Some girls develop eating disorders following sexual abuse. Girls with anorexia feel fat even when they are skinny. They simply do not see themselves as others see them. Anorexia may stop a girl's menstrual cycles.

Bulimia

Bulimia is the uncontrolled, rapid ingestion of large quantities of food, which occurs approximately twice a week, followed by vomiting, laxatives, or water pills for the purpose of weight control. Girls with bulimia seldom lose large amounts of weight. About 25 percent of girls with anorexia develop bulimia.

What Parents Can Do:

- Remember that children simply cannot stop an eating disorder without professional help. Strategies such as requiring a girl to eat only in front of you or promising rewards for successful weight gain will not work.
- Anorexia is a life-threatening eating disorder. Don't wait until the girl requests professional help before seeking intervention. Hospitalization may be necessary.
- Value her for qualities other than her accomplishments and appearance. For example, honor her problem-solving ability.
- Encourage the child to talk about feelings and accept negative feelings as well as positive ones.
- Encourage her to spend time with accepting and supportive friends.
- Don't argue with her denial of an eating problem, but lovingly state you believe she has a problem.
- Encourage her to make her own choices whenever possible.
- Tell her that she does not have to worry about you.
- Discourage the need to be the winner. Don't compare her score to others. Say, "Did you have fun doing this?"

▶ WHAT THE BIBLE SAYS:

1 Timothy 4:8   Training your body helps you in some ways, but serving God helps you in every way.

Hebrews 4:15-16   For our high priest is able to understand our weaknesses. When he lived on earth, he was tempted in every way that we are, but he did not sin. Let us, then, feel free to come before God's throne. Here there is grace. And we can receive mercy and grace to help us when we need it.

▶ WHAT TO SAY:

"I love you."

"I know that you feel embarrassed and ashamed about having anorexia and wish you could stop it. You deserve help."

"Here is a magazine article about another fifteen-year-old with anorexia. It has some ideas about what helped her."

"I know that it isn't helpful when I tell you how skinny you are and ask how much you have eaten. I am going to try to leave those concerns with you and your doctor. I know I can't control your eating."

"I don't need help with preparing supper. How about doing something fun instead?"

"Imagine yourself feeling confident, secure, and able to eat normally."

"I threw our bathroom scale away. You don't need the temptation to weigh yourself every day."

"Your friend Jenni seems so caring. I'm glad you have such a close friend."

"Here is a notebook you can use as a journal to write your feelings."

"Final exam week is coming up soon. That will add some extra stress. Let's plan some ways to take the pressure off you."

[Also see: Overweight; Self-esteem]

GOING TO THE HOSPITAL

What Children Might Experience and How Parents Can Help:

Before Being Hospitalized

WHEN A hospitalization is expected, tell the child one week prior to going to the hospital, and tour the hospital a day or so before admission. Talk about such things as bedpans, side rails, food trays, wheelchairs, and X rays.

- Ready the child's room at home for his return before he leaves for the hospital.
- Tell the child that in the hospital he must still obey and follow family rules.
- Be calm and reassuring, regardless of your doubts and fears. The attitude of the parent about the hospitalization will be felt by the child.
- Read books about hospital experiences of other children.

In an effort to soften the hospitalization, parents sometimes paint a positive picture and omit the pain and scary side. Telling a child she will get ice cream after surgery may be true but leaves the child unprepared for the bleeding, pain, and nausea.

During the Hospitalization:

- Children imagine that what is happening to the child in the next bed will also happen to them.

- They assume that pain from medical procedures is punishment for being naughty and should be told that nothing the child did caused the pain.

- Write a journal of daily happenings and take pictures of the child in the hospital, so that he can share the experience with friends when he is well.

- Children generally feel better in a room with other children, not in a private room.

- Don't threaten the child by telling her such things as "If you're not good, the nurse will give you a shot."

The child will be influenced by hearing about someone else's hospitalization and what happened to that person. The quality of time parents spend with the child is more important than the quantity. Parents must care for siblings at home, not just the sick child. Hospitalization offers a growth experience for children as they learn they can handle difficult situations.

▶ WHAT THE BIBLE SAYS:

Psalm 27:14   Wait for the Lord's help. Be strong and brave and wait for the Lord's help.

Psalm 91:11   He has put his angels in charge of you. They will watch over you wherever you go.

▶ WHAT TO SAY:

"You can wear your own pajamas except on the day of your operation."

"I'm crying because I feel sad that you have to go through this, but I can still take care of you."

"When you feel scared, you can choose to think a happy thought, like Jesus being right here with you."

"A nurse stays awake all night while you are sleeping. If you wake up and need something, she will come."

"I know that you can handle this."

"If you hear something you want to understand better, tell me. I will try to explain."

"The nurse will tell you the truth if something is going to hurt. Nobody is going to try to trick you."

"It's not being a baby to want your teddy bear while you are at the hospital. You'll give it up when you feel safe again."

"The doctor will need to examine all of your body, including your private parts. This touching is okay because it is for your health."

"I don't know what will happen next, but I know I will be right here with you."

"The nurse won't know that you are having pain. She expects you to tell her if you need some medicine for pain."

"I'm glad that we have a good doctor who knows how to help you."

"Would you like me to hold your hand while you get the shot? You can squeeze my hand really hard."

"This is not the kind of illness that makes people die. I think you will be home in a few days."

[Also see: Chronic Illness; Critical Illness]

LEARNING DISABILITY

What Parents Need to Know:

S OME VERY famous people had learning disabilities, including Thomas Edison, the inventor; Woodrow Wilson, the twenty-seventh president of the United States; and Albert Einstein, the physicist. Children with learning disabilities may have near average, average, or above average intelligence. A learning disability has nothing to do with whether a family is rich or poor or their race. Children with learning disabilities are sometimes called lazy, undisciplined, bored, uncontrolled, stubborn, mentally retarded, slow, emotionally disturbed, or spoiled. None of these words accurately describes a learning disabled child.

Characteristics of Learning Disabled (L.D.) Children:

- Early risers; poor sleepers; sleep at strange times
- Don't seem to understand the meaning of No!
- Get into everything
- Throw tantrums over nothing and act as though the whole world is against them
- Easily distracted; every noise or motion catches their eye
- Enjoy playing with other children but end up fighting or are left out because they don't understand the rules

- Don't show normal fear; for example, they may climb a tall tree
- Clumsy at tying their shoes or batting a ball; poor eye-hand control
- Can't remember where to go, get lost, lose belongings

More boys than girls have learning disabilities. There are many, many reasons why children are learning disabled, but knowing the cause doesn't mean there is a cure.

Help for Parents of a Learning Disabled Child:

- L.D. children need to hear over and over from many sources that they are intelligent and that although they need more time to learn things, they *will* make it in the world.
- Taking away a privilege works better than spanking a L.D. child.
- Children often don't understand what is expected or how to act in a social situation. Tell the child simply and clearly.
- Learning disabled children may have special talents. It helps build self-esteem to encourage these gifts.
- When giving instructions, get on the child's level and look the child directly in the eye.
- Have a regular routine for the L.D. child. He should get up and go to bed at the same time, for example.
- Teach other relatives, baby-sitters, and other adults about the child and how they can be helpful in their interactions with him.

Help for Brothers and Sisters:

L.D. children may have few friends so parents may expect siblings to share their time and friends with him. Taking a L.D. sibling along can be hard because he must be watched every minute, may destroy others' possessions, and doesn't know the rules to games.

Brothers and sisters may act mean or feel guilty for their negative feelings when they really do love their L.D. sibling. They can learn exceptional understanding and adapt, just as parents adapt.

▶ WHAT THE BIBLE SAYS:

Proverbs 1:7 Knowledge begins with respect for the Lord.

Romans 15:4 Everything that was written in the past was written to teach us, so that we could have hope.

Titus 3:14 Our people must learn to use their lives for doing good deeds. They should do good to those in need. Then our people will not have useless lives.

▶ WHAT TO SAY:

"He heard you, he just forgets immediately because of his learning disability."

"You are such a great helper."

"He likes it when you hug, smile, wink, or laugh with him."

"You are a very smart boy who sometimes fails at school because you have a problem. We can help you."

"People may think you are not paying attention, but, in fact, you are paying too much attention to too many things."

"Let me show you what I mean, rather than tell you."

"Give him one toy at a time."

"He has trouble making simple decisions. Don't pressure him."

"You have to obey the family rules just like everyone else."

"Of course he has chores. All the children in our family have chores."

"Jason, you interrupted your brother. I know that it is hard to wait for your turn to speak."

[Also see: Mental Retardation]

MENTAL ILLNESS

What Parents Need to Know:

BOTH CHILDREN and adults may become mentally ill and need the help of a professional. Sometimes the person who is sick does not know he needs help, or doesn't know that help is available.

Signs That a Person Is Mentally Ill:

- Excessive worry or fear that lasts a long time, and is not related to a normal frightening situation
- Severe and long-lasting depression, which includes: feelings of inadequacy, helplessness, and hopelessness; withdrawal from friends and enjoyable activities; difficulty sleeping; loss of appetite; constant tiredness
- Extreme changes in mood, behavior, or habits, unrelated to a recent event (A person who has always saved money suddenly spends large amounts, for example.)
- Physical sickness from worry and stress, such as severe tension headaches
- Aggressive, rude, or angry behavior over small incidents

What Makes People Mentally Ill:

- brain injury or infection

- drugs or alcohol
- inheriting an illness
- extreme stress
- changes in the blood chemistry
- environment
- some people have less ability to cope with stress than others

Kinds of Mental Illnesses:

1. Thought Disorders (such as schizophrenia):

   Schizophrenia is a serious mental illness with symptoms that begin between late teenage years and middle age. These people may have difficulty in relationships, in work, and in being able to take care of themselves. Some people with schizophrenia have false beliefs, hear or see things that aren't there, and withdraw from the real world to their own private thoughts.

2. Feeling Disorders (such as depression):

   One type of depression is *bipolar disorder*. The person with bipolar disorder alternates between excitement, hyperactivity, loud speech, and decreased need for sleep; and, at the other extreme, severe depression. The depressed person has difficulty finding pleasure or interest in his usual activities, feels hopeless, worthless, sad, and has difficulty sleeping.

3. Anxiety Disorders:

   There are many kinds of anxiety disorders, such as intense, irrational fears; panic attacks; post-traumatic stress disorders.

4. Personality Disorders:

   People with personality disorders have difficulty adjusting to the rules and expectations of society. These people may have difficulty learning from experience, may be impulsive, have sudden mood changes, and are unstable or suspicious.

Treatments for Mental Illnesses:

Treatments for mental illness include medication, talking to a professional (psychotherapy), electro-shock treatments, psychiatric hospitalization, recreation, marriage counseling, hypnosis, art therapy, drama, occupational therapy, and management techniques.

► WHAT THE BIBLE SAYS:

Philippians 4:6-7 Do not worry about anything. But pray and ask God for everything you need. And when you pray, always give thanks. And God's peace will keep your hearts and minds in Christ Jesus. The peace that God gives is so great that we cannot understand it.

1 Thessalonians 5:14 Encourage the people who are afraid. Help those who are weak. Be patient with every person.

► WHAT TO SAY:

"People who are mentally ill are sick, just like people with other kinds of illnesses."

"Would you like to go with me to visit Aunt Molly at the psychiatric hospital?"

"Please ask whatever questions you have about mental illness. If I don't know the answer, I will find out for you."

"Kids can help a mentally ill person by talking about what they are doing at school, going for a walk with the person, taking art to the room at the hospital, and by smiling and giving hugs, if the person is comfortable with that."

"How about writing a report for school on one of the types of mental illness?"

"People who love God can become mentally ill too. Being a Christian doesn't mean you won't get mentally sick."

"Let's pray for Laurie at the psychiatric hospital that her psychiatrist will know how to help her."

"I know that some people think Christians shouldn't take medicines

for mental illness, but they are wrong. God can use the medicine to help make them better."

"There are some things you can do to keep mentally healthy, such as not drinking alcohol or taking illegal drugs; talking about your feelings to someone who loves you; and asking for help when you have sad feelings that won't go away."

[Also see: Dementia; Mental Retardation]

MENTAL RETARDATION

What Children Need to Know:

- *Mental retardation* means that a person has lower than average intelligence. There is a wide range of retardation from mild to profound. A person who is mildly retarded can probably complete sixth grade while a profoundly retarded person will need a caretaker throughout life.

- About one out of ten families in the United States has a mentally retarded person in the immediate family.

- Retardation occurs for a variety of reasons. Sometimes babies are born retarded, and other times people become retarded due to brain injury, drugs, or other trauma. Often no one knows why a particular person is retarded.

- Parents may not know that a child is retarded until he is unable to learn what other children the same age are learning.

- Children can understand that not every family can manage the care needs of a retarded person in the home. Some families will place the person in a foster home, but this doesn't mean they don't love the retarded person as much as families who keep the person at home.

- There are many community organizations that can help the retarded person. The family is not alone. A person's worth is never based on how good-looking or how smart she is.

What Children Might Experience:

- Children can be taught basic skills in helping retarded friends: give simple directions one at a time; repeat the information over and over; praise the retarded child when he learns a new skill.

- Parents and children may feel sad, worried, or even guilty, but that does not mean they are not also proud and happy to have the retarded child in the family.

- The family principle of doing your best applies to all children in the family, including the retarded child.

- Children can be taught ways to help the retarded classmate, such as by including them in games at recess and by helping them with reading.

- Children need to be told that slang expressions such as "retard" are hurtful and should never be used. Children should show respect for all people.

What Parents Can Do:

- It is easy for parents of a retarded child to become preoccupied with the needs of the child and neglect one-on-one time with the other children.

- Mentally retarded children are not special. All children are special because they are children of God and He loves us all the same.

- Children learn to be comfortable around retarded persons by observing the Special Olympics, by reading books about retarded people, or by knowing adults who model friendships with retarded adults.

- Parents should be accepting of children who are embarrassed by the behavior of the retarded family member. Both the retarded person and siblings need to learn social skills that are acceptable.

▶ WHAT THE BIBLE SAYS:

Ecclesiastes 9:10 Whatever work you do, do your best.

Luke 20:21 "Teacher, we know that what you say and teach is true. You teach the same to all people. You always teach the truth about God's way."

▶ WHAT TO SAY:

"He is retarded. He is also an adorable little boy. Let's tell his mom we think he is cute."

"I noticed how patient and kind you were with Jeremy. I think you made God smile."

"I know that sometimes it is hard for you to have a retarded sister. I also know that you love her."

"Thank you for watching Jenny today so she wouldn't wander away or get hurt. Now it is my turn to watch her. You go play."

"You can teach your friends about mental retardation. You know a lot of good information that could help them."

"Retarded children play with toys for younger children."

"None of us is perfect. We all have difficulty doing some things and need the help of others."

"We don't know what will happen in the future for Bobby, just as we don't know what choices you will make. God will help us as we need him."

"Let's just take one day at a time."

"It is okay to be curious about mentally retarded people. I'd like to answer any questions you have."

"She has Down's Syndrome. I can tell by her facial features. You can't always tell by looking if someone is mentally retarded though."

"You can choose your attitude about what happens even if you can't change the situation."

"God didn't make your brother retarded. We live in a world where it can happen. God loves him and us."

"There are public laws that protect the right of mentally retarded children to have access to a good education."

[Also see: Dementia; Mental Illness]

ORGAN
TRANSPLANTS

What Children and Parents Need to Know:

CHILDREN NEED to know how their parents feel about organ donation because this provides a model for children in making their own ethical decisions. In particular, parents need to point out specific moral issues related to donation or transplants. Families may object to experimental transplants, such as those using animal organs, but not to proven transplant procedures.

Christians believe that at the time of death, the believer's soul goes to heaven and, therefore, there is no reason why the physical body cannot be used to help others here on earth. Every day people in the United States die while they wait for an organ transplant. And every thirty minutes the national transplant waiting list adds names. Organ transplants are unavailable for thousands of people each year, and even when they are available, many people cannot afford the medical care to receive a transplant. Insurance policies may cover nonexperimental transplants, but often people in need of a transplant lose their insurance due to chronic illness and their inability to work. The cost of a transplant may be as much as $200,000, and people without insurance are often asked to raise one-half of this money before the hospital will admit them for a transplant. Families with a child in need of a transplant may have an easier time raising the money for a transplant from the public than a middle-aged person would. The time it takes to raise money to get a transplant may be longer than a person can live without the transplant. Medicare pays for some kinds of transplants. There has been debate about whether people should be allowed to sell their organs, as they do in some other countries. Many people are afraid that the poor will sell organs to survive.

Why People Don't Donate Organs:

- They may be asked to do it in an insensitive way.
- There may be uncertainty in the minds of family members about whether taking an organ from a person on life-support machines will cause the person to die prematurely.
- It is hard for families to offer the gift of life to another person when their own loved one is dying.
- The decision to donate organs must be made under intense stress while a family member is alive on machines. The person will be declared dead at the conclusion of the transplant.
- Not everyone knows how much organs are needed.
- Even when families would like to donate organs, not every person has acceptable organs to give.
- It is not always clear to families when a person is dead and cannot be revived.
- Families do not know the recipient and do not want to give a loved family member's organs to a stranger.
- Families fear that donating an organ will be expensive.
- Families are not sure how the dying person would feel about organ transplant because they have never discussed it.

Some organs can be donated after death, such as bone, skin, and corneas, but most needed organs must be donated prior to termination of life-support machines that maintain heart and lung functioning.

Even if a family can raise the money for a transplant, it may not be able to afford the special medicines that are necessary afterwards, which sometimes cost $15,000 or more each year.

What Parents Can Do:

- Carry an organ donor card in your wallet. Show it to your children.
- Talk with family members about how you feel about organ donation.

▶ WHAT THE BIBLE SAYS:

1 Peter 1:5 God's power protects you through your faith, and it keeps you safe until your salvation comes.

1 Peter 1:23 You have been born again. This new life did not come from something that dies, but from something that cannot die. You were born again through God's living message that continues forever.

▶ WHAT TO SAY:

"When the Bible doesn't tell us specifically what to do about a particular decision, we use the principles of God's word. That's why we believe that one way to love other people, like God told us to do, is to allow our organs to be used after we die."

"We won't be needing those organs after we're dead because we'll be in heaven with perfect bodies."

"I hope someone would donate an organ for us if anyone in our family needed it."

"Let's pray for the family of the person whose organ is being donated. They are doing a wonderful thing, but they must be feeling very sad right now to have their loved one die."

"Giving to others is one way to show that we are Christians."

"Let's pray for the doctors and nurses who are doing the transplant using Uncle Joe's liver."

"God cares about everything that happens to us, including finding a bone marrow donor match for Jessica."

"I want you to know that I hope my organs can be used for transplant when I die."

[Also see: Chronic Illness]

OVERWEIGHT

WE LIVE in a culture that values being thin. Overweight children need to know that their worth doesn't depend on the bathroom scale. Children who are cherished are able to offset society's damaging prejudice.

Parents Can Support Overweight Children By:

- Helping them develop healthy lifestyle habits even if they never become thin.

- Finding athletic experiences which allow overweight children to successfully compete while having fun.

- Teaching children that ignoring people who tease them removes some of the taunter's power to hurt the child.

- Telling children that by being friendly and considerate of others they will be less likely to be teased about their weight.

- Spending the time and money for well-fitting and attractive clothing that will help children feel good about their appearance.

- Asking children if they want help from you in losing weight before intervening.

- Providing older children with the assistance of a hairstylist or make-up specialist to maximize natural appearance.

- Giving parties at home so children can invite others over, or allowing children to include a friend when the family goes to a basketball game. This provides a support system for the child.

- Teaching children that any diet should be supervised by a medical doctor. No fad diets. No fasting.
- Telling children that they should sit at the table for all meals and snacks. They should not eat while watching TV.
- Providing rewards other than sweets and other unhealthy foods.
- Giving children positive messages that are not related to eating, food, body size, or appearance.

Responsible parents provide regular meals and snacks, but that is where their control must end. Although only good foods should be available, it is the child, not the parent, who must decide how much to eat. Children should be offered as much good food as they want; otherwise, they may overeat out of fear that there won't be enough food for them. The child is the only real authority on his hunger.

What Parents Need to Know:

One-third of U.S. children under eighteen are considered overweight. If a child looks overweight, he is. Sixty to eighty-five percent of overweight children remain overweight throughout their lives. The longer children remain overweight as children, the more probable that they will be overweight adults.

Overweight is caused by eating more calories than are needed, but the tendency to gain easily is often an inherited one. Some children will have an uphill battle with weight control, even though they do everything right. Once overweight is established, dieting, counseling, exercise programs, or behavioral therapy may not demonstrate much success in maintaining significant long-term weight loss.

Overweight runs in families. If neither parent is overweight, there is a 7 percent chance that the child will be overweight. If both parents are overweight, there is an 80 percent chance the child will be overweight. The parents' eating and exercise habits influence the habits of the children. Between the ages of one and ten, boys are usually thinner than girls. As teenagers, girls usually gain more fat while boys lose fat. An overweight little girl will not lose her baby fat as a teenager. Nutrition experts state that patterns of overweight may be set by the time a child is between one and three years of age.

Cultural attitudes toward overweight vary in other countries. For example, in countries where food is scarce, overweight is a sign of status. In Western affluent cultures, thin is in.

Overweight children need to learn to respond to internal cues about when they are hungry instead of eating in response to stress, because food is available, everyone else is eating, they are bored, or it is time to eat. Even with highly motivated children, weight loss is difficult once a child is overweight. Weight can rarely be lost without a program of reduced fat intake, increased exercise, and much encouragement.

Some children will overeat as a defense against sexual abuse. Children who have been abused may attempt to protect themselves from adults by gaining extra weight. Children need to be affirmed every day for who they are, not how they look. Children with control in other areas of their lives will be less inclined to abuse food.

▶ WHAT THE BIBLE SAYS:

1 Corinthians 6:19: You should know that your body is a temple for the Holy Spirit. The Holy Spirit is in you.

Isaiah 43:4: You are precious to me. I give you honor, and I love you.

▶ WHAT TO SAY:

"I am sorry you were teased today. I wish I could protect you from the unkindness of people who don't understand how hard you work at losing weight."

"It's called junk food because it has so little nutritional value for your body."

"It is never okay to make fun of an overweight person."

"You don't need to lose weight for your mom and me to be proud of you. Our respect and appreciation of you doesn't have anything to do with your weight."

"Filling up on junk food will keep you from getting enough vitamins, minerals, and energy to do well in sports and in your school work."

"Would you take an exercise class with me? I need help in losing weight."

"I've sliced some apples for your after-school snack, if you are hungry."

"Would you like to learn some new recipes that are low fat? Let's fix dinner together tonight."

"I like the way you make good choices about what to eat. I think you are very smart."

"Let's go to the grocery store and you can help choose foods for the family."

"The whole family is going swimming this afternoon after we get our work done."

"Here is your new sticker chart for keeping track of doing your chores. We won't be using food as a reward anymore. When you complete the row, you can choose an activity that you think would be fun."

"The way we look on the outside is not as important as the way we look on the inside."

"I won't love you more if you lose weight, or be disappointed in you if you don't lose. "

PHYSICAL DISABILITIES

What Children Need to Know:

- People who have disabilities are not necessarily special, courageous, or brave. Some are, and some are not, just like the rest of us.
- Using a wheelchair doesn't always mean that a person is sick. (Children may have seen sick people sitting in wheelchairs at the hospital.)
- Not all hearing-impaired people can read lips.
- People who have disabilities are essentially the same as everyone else. They go to school, play, get their feelings hurt, have friends, get mad, and get sick.
- Disabled friends are gifted and are more skilled in some areas than the child. Able-bodied children can learn that they need help from their disabled friends at times.
- Some Christians make families feel bad by saying that if they really believed God could heal the disabled person, he could walk again. Children need to know that walking doesn't depend on a person's faith.
- It is good to pray for people with any kind of difficulty and know that God will always give the strength they need, if he does not heal them.
- Children must be taught how to interact empathetically with

a physically disabled person. Instead of telling the child to be quiet when he says something embarrassing in front of a disabled person, provide factual information about the disability and explain that unkind comments make them feel sad, just as they would for the child.

What Parents Need to Know:

Marriages are often stressed when there is a disabled family member. A disability doesn't make a marriage fall apart, but not talking about feelings will. Young children don't think of disabilities as something that could happen to them.

Parents of disabled children should plan ahead for especially difficult times, such as prom night or graduation.

Children may be frightened by a disability. Parents who model comfortable interactions will help lessen fear in children. Don't use the term *crippled*. It focuses on what the disabled person can't do instead of what they can do.

We live in a society that values beauty above almost anything else. Children need to know that this is not a Christian value.

Brothers and Sisters of Disabled Children May:

- Worry about their responsibility to their disabled sibling when their parents get older.
- Resent the family focus on the disabled child.
- Feel confused about what their parents expect from them. Is it okay to go out and play, or should they stay home and help? They need to be told specifically the expectations of the parents.
- Need to be told what will likely happen in the future with the disability. Is the disability progressive?
- Need focused attention that is separate from the disabled child. They need to have fun with friends and parents.

▶ WHAT THE BIBLE SAYS:

Philippians 3:21 He will change our simple bodies and make them like his own glorious body. Christ can do this by his power. With that power he is able to rule all things.

1 Peter 4:1 Christ suffered while he was in his body. So you should strengthen yourselves with the same way of thinking Christ had.

1 Peter 5:9-10 Stand strong in your faith. You know that your Christian brothers and sisters all over the world are having the same sufferings you have. Yes, you will suffer for a short time. But after that, God will make everything right. He will make you strong. He will support you and keep you from falling.

▶ WHAT TO SAY:

"It's not okay for us to park in the handicapped parking space. We will park wherever we find another spot."

"You can ask her the name of her disability. You just need to use good manners in asking."

"Not everyone with a disability needs help. You can say, 'If you need help please tell me.'"

"How about writing a paper for school about all the places that a person in a wheelchair couldn't enter, such as some classrooms at our church."

"When I heard my friend say she didn't want to invite Janet to the party because of her wheelchair, I told her she should invite Janet to the party if she liked her. Her wheelchair has nothing to do with friendship."

"It must hurt her feelings to have adults ask her mother, 'What does she want?' She is quite capable of speaking for herself."

Sexual
Topics

ABORTION

What Children Need to Know:

CHILDREN CAN be told that abortion is ending the life of an unborn child usually during the first twelve weeks of pregnancy. Abortion is not against the law in the United States, and it is usually done by a doctor at a clinic or a hospital when a woman requests it. Since abortion is highly controversial, children will sense the tension that surrounds the topic. Give them simple, age-appropriate, factual information. Children should be told what their parents believe and how they came to that conclusion regarding whether abortion is right or wrong.

What to Tell Children about Abortion:

- Many children will choose to express their beliefs to their friends, by writing school papers or participating in demonstrations. Children in middle school often have strong opinions about right and wrong. In one survey, children who were asked about the meaning of abortion said it meant, "killing a baby before it is born." In addition to encouraging children to take a stand on their beliefs, teach them to be sensitive and kind to others who have different beliefs. Children can learn to express their views without being offensive or hurtful to others.

- Children need to understand that a woman's feelings after

abortion are complex. A woman may have an abortion, but that does not mean that she will not feel deep sadness. Likewise, the choice to deliver the baby and place it for adoption does not mean the woman will not grieve. Usually after an abortion a woman feels a sense of relief along with the sad feelings. However, the hard grief often comes several years later.

- Junior high children can understand that there are a variety of situations in which abortion may be considered, such as when the life of the mother is in danger or following a rape. Some people do not believe in abortion on demand but do believe it could be used in certain situations.

- Adults need to be sensitive in describing an abortion to the child who asks, "How do they do it?" The process can be terrifying for a young child. A parent can say, "In an abortion, a doctor takes a baby out of the mother's uterus before it is ready to be born, so the baby dies."

- Children can be told that there is a difference of opinion about when an unborn baby is really a human being. Some people believe that the unborn baby is not a person until it can live outside of the mother. Other people believe that human life begins at conception and therefore abortion is murder.

- Tell children there are two groups of people. Those who are pro-choice believe the woman has the right to choose whether she will get an abortion. Pro-life people are against abortion.

- Children need to know that all people are loved by God, including people who get an abortion.

▶ WHAT THE BIBLE SAYS:

Psalm 139:13-16 You made my whole being. You formed me in my mother's body. I praise you because you made me in an amazing and wonderful way. What you have done is wonderful. . . . You saw my bones being formed as I took shape in my mother's body. When I was put together there, you saw my body as it was formed. All the days planned for me were written in your book before I was one day old.

Jeremiah 1:4-5 The Lord spoke these words to me: "Before

I made you in your mother's womb, I chose you. Before you were born, I set you apart for a special work."

▶ WHAT TO SAY:

"Getting an abortion because someone pressures you is dumb and wrong."

"In our family we believe that abortion is murder."

"Yes, having an abortion hurts unless some powerful medicine is used to prevent the pain."

"If your friend says that women have the right to control their own bodies, say, 'abortion is about the baby's body.'"

"Just because something is legal doesn't mean that it is right. Some bad laws need to be changed."

"Not every girl is mature enough to be a parent, but there are other choices available for her so her baby can live. Just because someone doesn't want a baby, doesn't mean the baby should die."

"The Bible teaches that life before birth is precious. Would you like me to read some verses about how God felt about you before you were born?"

"Let's take some baby clothes to the girl down the street who is pregnant."

"How do you feel about abortion?"

"It isn't okay to use bad manners with those demonstrators."

"Our family would like to help stop abortion. One way we can do this is to write letters to the leaders of our country and tell them we would like the abortion laws changed. You can sign the letter, too, if you want."

"There are many families that would like to adopt a baby, so if a woman can't be a parent, her baby can still have a good home. Let's look at the names of all the adoption agencies in the phone book."

[Also see: Adoption; Premarital Sex]

DIFFERENCES BETWEEN MEN AND WOMEN

S OME DIFFERENCES between men and women are genetic and some are learned. It isn't always easy to understand the source of a difference. Children hear teaching on the equality of men and women. They may fail to understand that men and women are *different* from each other, and that being equal does not mean that men and women are alike.

During late middle-school years, children will begin relating to the opposite sex in social experiences where gender roles are apparent, for example school dances and boys or girls sport teams. Since girls enter puberty before boys, there is often a disparity in physical and social maturity. Girls at this age often have better relational skills, are able to talk more deeply, resolve problems with friends with greater skill, and establish emotional closeness more easily.

What Children Need to Know:

- Neither boys nor girls should pretend they are not smart or good at a skill in order to impress someone of the opposite sex.

- Boys may not be interested in sports, and girls may excel in athletics. Boys are not always more physically aggressive. Some boys love to cook and are good at caring for little children.

- Boys are more likely to solve problems in a task-oriented way (guys go shopping to buy something and then go home). Girls solve problems with more focus on people and feelings (girls may go shopping to be with friends).
- Boys talk less than girls. Girls use three times as many words as boys beginning at about age two.
- Men and women may attain self-worth in different ways. Men feel good about themselves when they are successful in their work. Women are more likely to feel good about themselves when they are loved.
- Learning to make good friends with children of the opposite sex is very important. Dumb blonde jokes or male chauvinist pig jokes do not model respect.
- Although equality curriculum will be presented in schools, children may still be exposed to adult conversations about gender specific roles in work settings, such as girls should be nurses and boys should be fire fighters. Children should know that they can do whatever job they are prepared to do.

What to Tell Children about the Difference between Men and Women:

- Men and women have different genes. They are basically different.
- Women live longer than men by about three to four years.
- Women convert food to energy more slowly than men.
- The boney structure of men and women is different: women have a shorter head, broader face, and less protruding chin. Men's teeth last longer than women's.
- Women have larger stomachs, kidneys, breasts, livers, appendixes, thyroids, and smaller lungs.
- Women have different hormones. They can menstruate, get pregnant, and breast-feed babies. They have smoother skin, less body hair, and a layer of fat under their skin. They laugh and cry more easily than men. All of these traits are due to the hormonal differences.
- Women have 20 percent fewer red blood cells. Since these cells carry oxygen, women get tired more easily than men.

- Men are 50 percent stronger physically than women. They can lift heavier loads than women.
- Women's heart rates and blood pressure are lower than men's.
- Women can tolerate high temperatures better than men.

▶ WHAT THE BIBLE SAYS:

Genesis 1:27   So God created human beings in his image. In the image of God he created them. He created them male and female.

Genesis 2:18, 22-24   Then the Lord God said, "It is not good for the man to be alone. I will make a helper who is right for him." . . . Then the Lord brought the woman to the man. And the man said, "Now, this is someone whose bones came from my bones. Her body came from my body. I will call her 'woman,' because she was taken out of man." So a man will leave his father and mother and be united with his wife. And the two people will become one body.

▶ WHAT TO SAY:

"I like the way you are growing up. You are the kind of boy we always wanted."

"God made men and women to be different. That's why God said that it isn't good for a man to be alone. We need each other."

"If a boy doesn't like you because you are so smart, then he really is dumb."

"You can choose whatever you want to be when you are grown. We will support you and help you."

"Hormones can make a girl feel uptight before her period. That's the way it was for your mother and for your grandmother."

"Just because you're a boy doesn't mean you don't feel like crying sometimes. You don't have to act tough."

"In our family, jokes that make fun of women are not acceptable."

"I know she talks more about her feelings than you do. You can learn to put your feelings into words."

"He'll grow up. Give him time. Someday he will probably be married and have little boys of his own."

"This home is an 'equal opportunity employer.' Boys do dishes and help clean house, just like the girls."

HOMOSEXUALITY

HOMOSEXUALITY IS sexual attraction to persons of the same sex. In recent years, many people have stopped thinking of homosexuality as a disorder and now consider it an alternative lifestyle. Children need to understand that homosexual behavior is sin, according to God, and should not be included in school curriculum programs that celebrate diversity.

What Children Need to Know:

Children can be told that there are many theories about why a person becomes gay, including:

- Gay persons may be born with some difference in genetic inheritance.
- Prenatal hormonal influences in the second three months of pregnancy may impact sexual orientation.
- Childhood trauma or lack of bonding to the father during early years may result in homosexual orientation.
- Most researchers believe that there is no one single cause for homosexuality. It is apparently not a learned behavior, however, since there is little evidence that homosexual parents produce homosexual children.

A Christian View of Gay Rights:

- Persons who advocate for gay rights believe:

1. The law has an obligation to establish rules that guarantee the civil rights of gay persons.
2. Without special protection gay persons suffer loss of jobs and discrimination in housing.
3. It is unconstitutional to deny them special protection based on the moral beliefs of some people.
4. The gay movement believes that homosexuality is a normal, healthy choice, and that to believe otherwise is bigoted and can be compared to racial discrimination.

- Christians believe:
  1. The Bible is the standard for what is right or wrong.
  2. Homosexuality is a moral issue, and it is not okay to grant special rights for people who are doing something wrong, just as we would not give special rights to someone who is stealing or lying.
  3. Even if people are "born with it," homosexual behavior is not justified. Diabetes and alcoholism also have some genetic cause, but we do everything in our power to bring change so the person can live a normal life.
  4. There is a difference between having homosexual feelings and acting on those feelings. It is easier to stop actions than to stop thoughts and feelings.
  5. Christians are to love, support, help, and be friends with gay persons.
  6. Christians should not label others as gay because they wear one earring, because a guy likes art or cooking, or because the person has gay friends.
  7. It is not okay to try to change another person's sexual orientation by fixing him up with an opposite-sex date. It doesn't work, and it makes the gay person feel misunderstood. Just love, pray, and encourage professional counseling.

▶ WHAT THE BIBLE SAYS:

Romans 1:26-27 Because people did those things, God left them and let them do the shameful things they wanted to do. Women stopped having natural sex and started having sex with other women. In the same way, men stopped having natural sex and began wanting each other. Men did shameful things with other men. And in their bodies they received the punishment for those wrongs.

1 Corinthians 6:18 So run away from sexual sin. Every other sin that a man does is outside his body. But the one who sins sexually sins against his own body.

Jude 1:7 Also remember the cities of Sodom and Gomorrah and the other towns around them. They acted as the angels who did not obey God. Their towns were full of sexual sin and men having sexual relations with men. They suffer the punishment of eternal fire, as an example for all to see.

▶ WHAT TO SAY:

"Some Christian homosexuals feel their sin is worse than the sins of other people, but that's not true. God loves the homosexual as much as he loves you and me."

"God's plan was that a husband and wife have sex. Any other sexual relationship outside of marriage is wrong, whether it is homosexual or heterosexual."

"God will help a person who wants to stop homosexual behavior just like he helps you and me with our problems."

"Sometimes homosexual persons become heterosexual through the help of a counselor. Usually the person always feels homosexual but learns to obey God no matter how he feels."

"I know this is a hard subject to talk about. Please ask anything you wonder about. Curiosity is normal."

"There are lots of Bible verses about homosexual behavior. Would you like me to help you find them?"

"Our church has a support group for homosexuals. I'm taking cookies to their meeting so they know we love them and care about their struggles."

[Also see: AIDS; Prejudice]

MASTURBATION

MASTURBATION IS a normal activity and does not harm children, although like any activity it may become an excessive habit that is hard to break. Most children touch their genital organs for the good feelings it brings from the time they are about one to six years of age and again during teenage years. It is estimated that around 90 percent of adolescent boys and 60 percent of adolescent girls masturbate.

What Children Need to Know:

Jesus didn't talk about masturbation, but he did talk about lust (Matt. 5:28). Lust is thinking about a person you aren't married to in a sexual way. Teenagers may have feelings of lust while they masturbate. Jesus said this is wrong.

Children can be told that although the Bible does not specifically talk about masturbation, we can rely on the general principles of Scripture in adopting a Christian view of the subject. For example:

- God understands all of our feelings.
- God made our bodies to work as they do.
- God can help us stop behavior when we can't stop by ourselves.
- God forgives us when we tell him we are sorry for our behavior and ask his help in changing.
- It is not okay to masturbate in front of other people.

- It is not okay to touch the genitals of other people.
- At times it may be necessary for a doctor or parent to touch the child's genitals, but it will only be done when the child needs medical care or because a very young child needs help with washing his or her genitals.

What Parents Can Do:

Some children masturbate as a result of having been sexually abused; they become overly sexual for their age. A parent who is concerned about the amount of time the child spends masturbating should describe the child's behavior clearly to the pediatrician. Children are especially likely to masturbate at bedtime, when they are bored, when they watch TV, or when they are listening intently to a story.

Children may masturbate excessively because:

- They are forced to spend too much time in their bedrooms as a form of punishment.
- They are sent to bed too early.
- They have inadequate sources of pleasure.
- They are under stress and are seeking self-comfort.

Since grandparents are often from the era in which masturbation was falsely believed to cause mental illness, stunt growth, cause sexual problems as adults, or cause blindness, they may strongly disapprove of parents' casual attitude toward masturbation.

- Distract the child to another activity, especially one that includes appropriate interacting with others.
- Help children develop more active play and fun.
- Teach children social skills to enlarge their circle of friends.
- Give children something to hold when taking a nap, such as a soft toy.
- Tell children that masturbating may be done only when they are alone in their rooms, then set limits on how much time they spend there.

- Recognize that excessive masturbation may be a symptom of a more serious problem.

- Do not allow children to observe parents in any sexual interaction.

- Supervise children who are playing alone. Leave doors open.

- Answer questions about body parts simply and without embarrassment. This removes some of the mystery about differences between boys and girls.

- Boys need to know that they may experience ejaculation as a result of masturbating. Also, nocturnal emissions (wet dreams) are normal and occur while a boy is asleep.

▶ WHAT THE BIBLE SAYS:

Matthew 5:27-28 "You have heard that it was said, 'You must not be guilty of adultery.' But I tell you that if anyone looks at a woman and wants to sin sexually with her, then he has already done that sin with the woman in his mind."

1 Corinthians 6:12 "I am allowed to do all things." But all things are not good for me to do. "I am allowed to do all things." But I must not do those things that will make me their slave.

1 Corinthians 6:19-20 You should know that your body is a temple for the Holy Spirit. The Holy Spirit is in you. You have received the Holy Spirit from God. You do not own yourselves. You were bought by God for a price. So honor God with your bodies.

▶ WHAT TO SAY:

"I noticed that you were playing doctor with Jaime. I can understand that you are curious about her body parts, but it is not okay to touch her. I will show you some pictures in a children's book that will help you understand how boys are different from girls."

"I'm not mad at you for masturbating."

"Let's invite Joel over and go to the park to play. You have been alone a long time."

"Grandma is learning new facts about masturbation. Sometimes people say wrong things because they don't know any better."

"I will quietly remind you not to touch yourself when there are other people around. I don't want you to be embarrassed."

"When you are bored you can tell me. Together we will try to figure out something else for you to do."

"When you feel like touching yourself during your nap, you can rub this soft toy."

"She masturbates too much because she was sexually abused. She deserves help. It is hard to stop this kind of problem alone."

[Also see: Sexual Abuse]

PREMARITAL SEX

THE PRIMARY sex education of children is the parents' model of respectful behavior with each other, their conversation in the home about marriage, their responses to sexual situations on TV, and their attitudes to unmarried, pregnant teenagers. These behaviors communicate the family values.

However, parents also need to talk to kids about sex. One survey found that 85 to 95 percent of parents of children under eleven have never talked to them about sex. Nearly 25 percent of fifteen-year-olds and 50 percent of nineteen-year-olds are sexually active.

Parents who are uncomfortable or ill-prepared to talk openly about sex can take classes on communicating with middle-school children about sexual issues, read books on the topic, and admit to children that they are unsure how to express their beliefs but want to talk about it because it is so important. The topic of sex before marriage should be discussed in grade school, not junior high. Two in ten unmarried teenage girls become pregnant and one-half of them abort.

What Parents and Children Need to Know:

Children need to know that there are many good reasons to wait until they are married to have sex:

- They won't likely get sexually transmitted diseases, including AIDS, if they are a virgin, marry a virgin, and remain faithful throughout the marriage.

131

- They won't get pregnant, which might require leaving school to take care of the baby or to work or placing the baby for adoption, which will cause sadness.
- Most teen relationships don't last, so the father of the baby will probably leave.
- Having sex before you are married makes most girls feel used, especially after the couple breaks up.
- Once a person starts having sex, he or she will usually continue to have sex in all future relationships unless a determined choice is made to stop.
- Sex is worth waiting for! A person has a lifetime to enjoy sex after marriage.
- Since God has said that sex before marriage is wrong, he gives people who want to obey him the power to wait for sex.
- It is insulting to think that people are at the mercy of their hormones, like dogs. *Of course* people are capable of controlling their sex drive.
- Sex has a way of taking over in a relationship. Once a couple starts having sex, they usually talk less to each other.
- The only way to know for sure that a person is interested in you as a person is if he or she is not having sex with you, and still wants to be with you.
- It helps teenagers to spend time with other teens who also want to obey God in their sexual behavior.
- Using a condom does not always prevent pregnancy, AIDS, or other sexually-transmitted disease.
- The only birth control method that is 100 percent effective is abstinence from intercourse.
- Problems associated with teen pregnancy include a higher risk of the baby dying, prematurity, and neurological problems in the baby.

Reasons Teenagers Give for Being Sexually Active:

- rebellion against parents
- lack of information about sex
- wanting someone (a baby) to love them

- wanting to be an adult
- sexual desire
- believing it was expected of them by peers
- low self-esteem: "He wouldn't want me if I didn't"

What Parents Can Do:

- Set strict guidelines about what is and is not acceptable behavior. A teen is not to entertain the opposite sex in a bedroom with the door closed, for example.
- Be warm and affectionate.
- Discourage early single dating and encourage going out with a group. Have parties at your home.
- Don't ask children in grade school if they have a boyfriend or a girlfriend.
- Tell children that although society may accept permissive sexual standards for boys, God's command to avoid sexual sins applies to boys as well as girls.
- Children are usually sexually mature by twelve years of age, but not married until their early twenties. They need to be taught what to do with their sexual drive. They can:
  1. Talk honestly about sexual temptations with a friend who will encourage chastity.
  2. Avoid situations that invite sexual acting out, such as going to parties where alcohol will be served and adults will not be present.
  3. Be faithful in church attendance.
  4. Avoid media that encourages sex.
- Use correct terminology for body parts.
- Don't wait for your middle-school child to bring the subject of sex into a conversation.
- Answer specifically what the child asks, and invite more questions.

▶ WHAT THE BIBLE SAYS:

1 Corinthians 10:13 The only temptations that you have are the temptations that all people have. But you can trust God.

He will not let you be tempted more than you can stand. But when you are tempted, God will also give you a way to escape that temptation. Then you will be able to stand it.

Hebrews 13:4 Marriage should be honored by everyone. Husband and wife should keep their marriage pure. God will judge guilty those who take part in sexual sins.

▶ WHAT TO SAY:

"It takes more courage to say No than to say Yes. I'm really proud of your choice."

"Everybody's not doing it."

"It is really hard to stop having sex once you start."

"Safe sex is sex that begins with virgins and remains between those two people for the rest of their lives."

"When they told you sex was safe if you use a condom, they were lying."

"Anyone that asks you to have sex after you have said No cares more about themselves than about you."

"We believe in waiting until marriage to have sex, but you might hear at school that you should just wait until you are in love or until you are ready. That's not what God says."

"I'm glad that you asked that question. I don't know the answer, but I'm going to look it up so you'll have accurate information."

"Your dad and I do not talk about our sexual relationship except with each other."

"Some people think that it's okay for guys but not girls to have sex before they are married. God doesn't have different rules for guys, though."

[Also see: Abortion]

PROTECTION AGAINST SEXUAL ABUSE

What Parents Can Do:

- Teach the child correct terms for all body parts so that if a child needs to report wrong touches, he can tell you accurately.

- Create a relaxed, matter-of-fact atmosphere for talks about sexual issues.

- Don't wait until your child asks about the danger of sexual abuse to talk about it.

- Give information in the context of general safety; health safety in not touching needles; traffic safety in riding a bike; and people safety involving people who might want to sexually touch the child.

- Children need specific information so they know exactly what to do if they are in an uncomfortable or scary situation.

- By the time a child is four years old, he is old enough to know your home phone number, how to call for help in an emergency, and how to place a collect call.

- Telling children to stay away from strangers is not enough to protect your child against sexual abuse since 90 percent of child abuse is committed by someone the child knows. The focus of teaching should be on the *behaviors* that are inappropriate, not the *person* who does it.

What Children Need to Know:

- Although parents wish they could always protect children from harm, children must learn to protect themselves when the parent is not present.
- Talking about sex is for private times at home with parents. It is not okay to talk about sex with other adults without the permission of the parents.
- Children need actual role-play practice in responding to inappropriate sexual advances. "What if . . ." games are helpful.
- Young children believe that a stranger is someone who looks like a bum, so stranger-danger talks are often unhelpful.
- Children should know that it is wrong for an adult to ask for help from a child. If adults need directions or help locating a lost puppy, they should not ask children. Adults ask adults for help.
- It is wrong for adults (other than parents or medical staff) to touch the child anyplace which would be covered by a swim suit, or for a child to touch an adult in that area.
- It is wrong for an adult to ask a child to keep any secret from the child's parents.
- Children should know that it is okay to say No to an adult who asks them to do something they have been told not to do by their parents, no matter what the adult says. For example, an adult might say, "Your mom told me to bring you home" or "Your dad is sick and sent me to get you."
- Children should know they are never to get in a car or van with anyone without the permission of their parents.

▶ WHAT THE BIBLE SAYS:

Ephesians 6:11-13 Wear the full armor of God. Wear God's armor so that you can fight against the devil's evil tricks. Our fight is not against people on earth. We are fighting against the rulers and authorities and the powers of this world's darkness.

We are fighting against the spiritual powers of evil in the heavenly world. That is why you need to get God's full armor.

▶ WHAT TO SAY:

"Grown-ups don't have the right to do anything they want with children. If an adult asks you to do something you feel funny about, just say, 'I have to ask my Dad about this first.'"

"There is a very sad story in the newspaper today about a little girl who was sexually hurt by someone she trusted. I'm glad that you know those touches are wrong, no matter who does it."

"Sex between married people is wonderful. Sexual abuse is terrible."

"I am so proud of you for telling me that your friend's dad made you feel funny in the way he talked to you."

"If you are ever lost, tell a police officer or someone at the checkout counter at the store that you need help finding your mom or dad."

"If someone tries to take you some place, scream really loud and say, 'I don't know this person.'"

"It isn't safe for you to walk home alone. How about walking with Jeff?"

"You don't have to kiss an adult you feel uncomfortable around, even if they are a relative."

"It isn't okay for adults you don't know to take pictures of you."

"I am glad that you told me you don't like Uncle Ted. Has something happened that made you uncomfortable?"

"If anyone says, 'Don't tell,' or, 'It's our secret,' or 'Your mom would be mad if you told her about this,' you should tell me right away. It's not okay for adults to say those things to children."

[Also see: Fears and Worries; Sexual Abuse]

SEXUAL ABUSE

SEXUAL ABUSE is common. The child who has not been sexually abused will have friends who have been abused, since it is estimated that one in three girls and one in four boys are sexually abused before they are eighteen years old. Eighty to ninety percent of children are abused by someone the child knows, not by a stranger.

What Parents Need to Know:

Sexual Abuse Includes:

- Adult nudity in front of the child
- Masturbating while the child watches
- Allowing the child to see pornographic videos
- Intimate kissing
- Touching the child's sexual organs or asking the child to touch the adult's
- Taking sexual pictures of the child
- Allowing the child to watch adults having sex
- Oral, anal, or vaginal penetration of the child

Simply stated, sexual abuse is any touch or behavior that has to be kept secret.

The child is usually not forced. The sexual abuse is generally gradual and based on a trusting relationship with an adult who has power over the child. Once sexual abuse begins, it generally will last three or more years. Most children make repeated attempts to communicate that they are in need of help. They may say they don't want to have a certain baby-sitter or go camping with Grandpa.

How to Know If a Child Is Being Sexually Abused:

- The child has sexual knowledge beyond his or her years.
- The child is uncomfortable around a previously trusted adult.
- The child has inappropriate sexual behavior with younger children or masturbates excessively.
- The child has eating problems, school problems, or sleeping problems, or is afraid, angry, or sad.
- The adult may not know for sure that the child is being sexually abused. If you suspect abuse, you should call the Children's Protective Services agency in your community and they will investigate.

Sexual Abuse in Boys:

- Boys are more likely to be abused outside of the family and by another male.
- Boys suffer from self-identity issues, such as: Am I a homosexual? What was different about me that made him choose to abuse me?
- Boys are more likely to be abused at a younger age than girls.
- Boys are more likely to be physically hurt in the abuse.
- Boys are less likely to talk about what happened. It is hard for boys to see themselves as victims, since they are supposed to be tough and take care of themselves.

Sexual Abuse in Girls:

- Girls are more likely to be abused by a male relative.
- The long-range impact of sexual abuse for girls includes difficulties trusting men in intimate adult relationships, shame, and damaged self-worth.
- The average age for sexual abuse to begin in girls is eight.
- There is frequently no physical evidence of sexual abuse in girls.

- Girls may not disclose the abuse until they are no longer living with the abusive family member.

What the Nonoffending Parent Can Do:

- Tell the child that they were brave to have told you what happened and that you will help protect her from being abused again.

- Since persons are legally innocent until proven guilty in a court of law, the accused family member may be allowed to remain in the home. The child may need to stay somewhere else temporarily to protect the child from contact with the accused offender.

- Say, "I'm so sorry this happened to you. I love you and will help you."

- Don't be surprised if your child is angry with you. Children think their parents could have protected them from the abuse. Say, "I didn't know this was happening."

- Tell the child that you will have to tell some other people so the abuse will stop.

- Don't express your rage at the offender in front of the child. Say, "Your uncle knew that what he was doing to you was wrong. It is never okay for a grown-up to touch a child sexually."

How an Adult Friend Can Respond to Disclosure of Sexual Abuse:

- If a child confides that he or she is being sexually abused, say, "I believe you and will help you." Report the abuse to the authorities before you allow the child to go home, where the child will probably tell their parents, who may talk them out of reporting to avoid the embarrassment.

- Be warm, but calm, as you listen to the child. Children are frightened by hysterical adults and a child may assume that they—rather than the perpetrator—have caused you to be upset. Don't ask for details of the abuse.

- Don't confront the offender. Leave that to the authorities.

- Call the police or the local Children's Protective Services. You can remain anonymous unless the case goes to court (which is rare).

- You can't be sued for reporting a suspicion if you are wrong as long as you report with good intent.
- Not every mother will believe the child. Some will take the side of the accused offender.

▶ WHAT THE BIBLE SAYS:

Ecclesiastes 8:14 But sometimes something senseless happens on earth. Bad things happen to good people. Good things happen to bad people. This is truly senseless.

Matthew 18:5-6 "Whoever accepts a little child in my name accepts me. If one of these little children believes in me, and someone causes that child to sin, then it will be very bad for that person. It would be better for him to have a large stone tied around his neck and be drowned in the sea.

Luke 18:15-17 Some people brought their small children to Jesus so that he could touch them. When the followers saw this, they told the people not to do this. But Jesus called the little children to him and said to his followers, "Let the little children come to me. Don't stop them, because the kingdom of God belongs to people who are like these little children. I tell you the truth. You must accept God's kingdom like a little child, or you will never enter it!"

▶ WHAT TO SAY:

"I believe you. I know you wouldn't make up something like this."

"You aren't responsible for making an adult do the right thing. He knows better."

"You don't have to have sex to get hugs and special attention. You deserve hugs just for being you."

"You can decide whether to tell your best friends about the abuse."

"The doctor will have to check your anus or vagina. I know that will be hard, but the doctor knows you didn't cause the abuse."

"I know that you like him and are angry with him at the same time."

"It doesn't mean that a boy is a homosexual when a man has sex with him. It's the man who has the problem, not the boy."

"Nobody can tell by looking at you that you have been sexually abused."

"I am going to take you to a counselor who knows how to help children who have been sexually abused."

"I know you feel guilty for not telling me about the sexual abuse sooner. You told when you could."

"I know that you feel confused, and embarrassed, and sad, and worried now. You won't always feel this way."

[Also see: Protection against Sexual Abuse; Masturbation]

WHERE DO BABIES COME FROM?

EIGHTY-FIVE percent of junior high students state that they did not receive sex education from their parents. They received sex education; they just didn't receive it from their parents.

The secrecy that surrounds the topic of sex in many Christian homes, coupled with warnings about chastity may cause children to believe that sex is nasty. Balancing the wonder, fun, and delightful passion that God planned for sex with communicating that sex outside of marriage is wrong is one of the great challenges of parenting. Christian parents may believe that if children don't know about sex, they won't get into trouble, or that sex education will come naturally when they need the information. Neither of these beliefs is true. Understanding sex is a lifelong process, and parents are the most important sex educators. By the time they are two or three, most children will have asked at least one question about sex.

What Children Need to Know:

By five years of age, a child should know:

- The correct name for all sexual body parts of both males and females. They should be able to talk about them without feeling that the talk is naughty.
- How boys and girls are physically different.

- That their sexual parts are private, and that they can say No to unwanted touching of their sexual parts, even by an adult.
- How babies "get in" and "get out" of the mommy.
- That it is okay to ask their parents questions about sex, but not other people.

By eight years old, a child should know:

- That babies require much care and that parents are responsible to take care of them.
- That all living things reproduce.
- That God made us sexual people and what is normal throughout the life cycle; for example, that a baby boy touches his penis for the good feeling; what happens at puberty; that grandparents enjoy married sex.
- That it is okay to talk to the school counselor or the pediatrician about sexual concerns.
- The names of common sexually transmitted diseases and how they are spread, including AIDS.
- What pornography, prostitution, sexual abuse are and that they are common sexually inappropriate behaviors.
- How to accurately discuss menstruation and wet dreams.
- What to do if approached sexually by an adult.
- What God says about family roles.

By twelve years old, a child should know:

- That sexual feelings are good, normal, and can be controlled.
- That sex is for enjoyment and closeness as well as for having a baby, and that most married couples use some form of birth control.
- What abortion is, how it is done, and why it is wrong.
- Details about normal pregnancy, delivery, and breast-feeding.
- That condoms do not provide safe sex.
- That TV and music may influence sexual thoughts and behavior.

- How to combat peer pressure to have sex.
- How to build and maintain healthy relationships with the opposite sex and when dating will be allowed.
- Problems that result from having sex prior to marriage and problems raising children as an unwed parent.

What Parents Can Do:

Children of any age should not observe their parents having sex. Young children may believe that "Daddy is hurting Mommy."

Children cannot understand the moral implications of sex until they are in the fourth or fifth grade.

Parents should talk about sex in a casual, comfortable way and clarify the child's question before answering it. The child who asks, "Where did I come from?" may receive a long discussion about sex before his *real* question is heard, "Did I come from Chicago, or where?"

Children need to know that sex in marriage was God's idea.

Sex education begins when the parent changes the diapers of a baby and grimaces, which babies may misinterpret as disgust for their genitalia

Children are literal thinkers. An appropriate way to explain sex to a three-year-old is, "Mommy and Daddy lie real close and love each other and then Daddy puts a special seed out of his penis into Mommy's vagina. The seed and the egg join to make a baby, which grows until it is big enough to live outside of Mommy. The baby is born through Mommy's vagina." Although this is an acceptable way to describe sex, most three-year-old children will think of the mommy's egg as being like a chicken's egg, and daddy's seed as being like a peach pit. "God brought you into our family" is true, but it is evasive and inappropriate for sex education.

Practice out loud what you want to say to your children about sex.

Ask children what they understand before and after your explanation.

If a child does not ask any sexual questions, initiate the discussion. Use pets for examples, or read library books about sex.

Talking in the car is often less embarrassing for the parent and the child since eye contact can be avoided.

Use pamphlets available from the doctor which show pictures of unborn babies.

Don't separate sexual and spiritual issues.

Frequent questions:

1. If the child asks, "Do you have sex?" The parent can say, "Grown-ups don't talk about their sexual behaviors with their children. It is private talk for Mommy and Daddy."

2. "If I tell my kids about sex, won't they try to do it?" No, say, "Sex is something that God made for married people."

3. "Should I let my child watch the birth of our baby?" Young children may be frightened by the blood at delivery and Mommy's groaning. After seven or eight years of age, another adult can stay with the child and explain what is happening during delivery. Many parents choose to allow children into the room as soon as the delivery is over.

▶ WHAT THE BIBLE SAYS:

Genesis 2:24-25 So a man will leave his father and mother and be united with his wife. And the two people will become one body. The man and his wife were naked, but they were not ashamed.

▶ WHAT TO SAY:

"We cover up our private parts, but it's not because they are bad. We do it because they are so special and not for everyone to see."

"Choosing someone to share your body with is a big decision that grown-ups make when they decide to get married."

"God doesn't want us to have sex before we get married because he doesn't want us to do something that is wrong for us and that disobeys his rule."

"What are some questions about sex that kids your age wonder?"

'Sex is much more than doing something physical. It is also loving one person in a special way for all of your marriage."

"Some kids will say that it is okay to have sex before you get married, but that is not true. God said to wait."

Emotional
Topics

DEATH OF A PARENT

YOUNG CHILDREN believe that their parents are all-powerful and can protect them. It is the only way to feel secure when you are totally dependent. So, when a parent dies, the sense of abandonment is monumental. In a survey of children ages eight to fourteen, the number one fear expressed by children was that a parent would die.

What Children Might Experience:

When a parent dies, a child often experiences the loss of both parents—one to death and the other to grief, at least for awhile. In addition, if the father dies, the child's mother may take a new job and be absent from home. If the mother dies, the child may have a new caregiver. The child's reaction to the death of a parent may be delayed. Young children cannot comprehend the impact of the death on their future life.

Developmentally, children do not understand that death is final until they are about nine or ten years old. Children may develop a fantasy about the dead parent. The parent may be perceived as having unrealistic qualities of sainthood.

When a parent dies, children are often the forgotten ones. The focus of comfort is usually on the surviving parent, and the grief of children is minimized.

All children wish temporarily their parents would die. Since children cannot differentiate the wish from the deed, they may feel guilty for their angry thoughts. In addition, children may have a sense of relief when a chronically ill parent dies, and this, too, will result in feelings of guilt.

What Children Need to Know:

- Children should understand the difference between minor illness and fatal illness.
- The child's questions should be answered in simple, literal answers. For example, Daddy didn't pass away, he died.
- Children need to know what they can do to help, and that their help is valued. In addition, children need permission to not help. They should play without guilt, go to birthday parties, and continue their lives.
- That even though adults around them are sad and crying, they can still take care of the children.
- Everybody handles feelings in their own way. How the child feels is her way of coping. All feelings are okay.
- The news of the parent's death is best given by the surviving parent.
- Children can accept the reality of the death more easily when there has been some preparation prior to the death, such as, "The doctor is doing everything possible to help your mom, but she is getting sicker." When death is near, children need to be told that the adults expect the person to die, but that medicine will help their parent stay comfortable.

▶ WHAT THE BIBLE SAYS:

Psalm 27:10 If my father and mother leave me, the Lord will take me in.

1 Corinthians 15:21-23 Death comes to everyone because of what one man did. But the rising from death also happens because of one man. In Adam all of us die. In the same way, in Christ all of us will be made alive again. But everyone will be raised to life in the right order. Christ was first to be raised. When Christ comes again, those who belong to him will be raised to life.

▶ WHAT TO SAY:

"Usually when people get sick, the doctor can help make them better. Being sick doesn't always mean a person will die."

"When a person is dead, they can't feel anything, and they don't eat or go to the bathroom. Once a person is dead, they don't come back to life."

"Your mom would have wanted you to play and have fun. She knew that is what children need to do."

"Yes, we will pray that God will make your daddy get well. Sometimes God says Yes to our prayers and sometimes he says No. No matter what happens, God loves us and will help us."

"Would you like me to tell you what the Bible says about heaven?"

"You can ask anything."

"God didn't make this happen. It happened because we live in a world that has cancer cells."

"Being dead is not the same as going to sleep. When you go to sleep, you wake up. You don't wake up from being dead."

"Your mommy's death isn't contagious. I think your daddy will live until he is old, like a grandpa."

"Your mom did not want to leave you. She wanted to stay alive and be your mommy."

"I know that you wonder what will happen next. When I know, I will tell you, and when I don't know, I will tell you that too."

"Lots of children feel angry when their parent dies. Feeling angry is normal. It is what you do with your angry feelings that is important."

"I can't promise that no one else in your family will die, but I can promise that you will always be loved and there will be someone to take care of you. You'll never be alone."

"I know that you were angry at Daddy sometimes, but you didn't make him die by being mad at him."

[Also see: Critical Illness; Fears and Worries; Funerals; Murder]

FEARS AND WORRIES

I T IS normal for children to be afraid when they imagine themselves to be in danger, or when they actually are in danger. Fear protects children from potential harm. Some of the fears result from parents teaching their children to be afraid, such as not crossing the street without looking both ways for cars. Fear is generally related to a specific object. Some children experience a vague, general uneasiness, which is called anxiety. A phobia is an irrational fear.

What Children Might Experience:

Parents May Increase Fear in Children:

- By threatening the child with fearful consequences for noncompliance with the parent's request, such as "If you don't take your medicine, the nurse will give you a shot."
- By unrealistic expectations of the child, "You better bring home all As on your report card."
- By making fun of the child's fears, such as, "Your brother was five when he learned to swim, and you're afraid of the water at ten?"
- By overprotection of mothers, "You can stay home from school today if you are that scared."
- By not taking the child's fears seriously, "Oh, you'll be fine. There is nothing to be afraid of."

- By excessive warnings, "If you don't come right home from school, I'll call the police and see if you have been kidnapped."

The types of fears a child has are usually age related. However, fearfulness may also be increased due to the child's personality type or gender.

Girls Express More Fears Than Boys:

- Girls are given more warnings about things to fear.
- It is more acceptable for girls to express fear.
- Boys may be just as afraid, but hide their fear by psychosomatic illness and emotional problems.

Children have the greatest number of fears in first through third grade. Their fears might include large dogs, the dark, monsters, deep water, nightmares, doctors, and death.

Children Are More Likely to Be Afraid If:

- They lack self-confidence.
- They have few sources of adult comfort.
- They have models of fearful adults.
- They are exposed to repeated frightening experiences such as horror movies on TV.
- Their fears are minimized, ignored, or taunted by adults.
- They are under stress.

What Parents Can Do:

- Children who are terrified of deep water should not be thrown into the deep end of the pool, and children who are afraid of large dogs should not be dragged kicking and screaming to a dog. Fears increase, rather than decrease, with such tactics. Allow children time to gradually get used to frightening circumstances without pushing them. Let children who swim play in the deep end of the pool with an adult before expecting them to swim alone in water over their heads.
- Building self-confidence in children gives them a sense of being able to handle difficult situations.

- Giving children information about how to handle scary situations is helpful, such as how to approach a strange dog.
- Provide a safe atmosphere for children to express their fears by asking how they feel in a situation and then communicating that you care about their fear, "That must be hard for you."
- Read stories of other children who were afraid and learned to handle their fears.
- Tell children that it is okay to be afraid, that you are afraid sometimes too.
- If irrational fear persists, seek professional help from a child psychologist.
- Don't lie to children by saying there is nothing to fear when adults are afraid also. Tell them what all of you can do about your fear: Stay together; ask for help; get more information.

▶ WHAT THE BIBLE SAYS:

Psalm 27:1   The Lord is my light and the one who saves me. I fear no one. The Lord protects my life. I am afraid of no one.

Proverbs 29:25   Being afraid of people can get you into trouble. But if you trust the Lord, you will be safe.

John 14:27   I leave you peace. My peace I give you. I do not give it to you as the world does. So don't let your hearts be troubled. Don't be afraid.

▶ WHAT TO SAY:

"Would you like to write a letter to the newspaper to say how scary it is to have the gang-shooting in our neighborhood? It might help other grown-ups know how kids feel."

"We have never had a tornado in our area. It is not likely to ever happen here."

"When you are afraid of something, I hope you will tell us. We want to help you."

"I know that you are worried about failing that test. Let me help you study for it, so you will feel prepared."

"Giving a speech is hard for many people. Some things that help are taking a few slow, deep breaths before you begin, and looking at the face of someone in the classroom who is your friend."

"When you have a nightmare, pretend your brain is a TV and you are changing the channel to a happy story."

[Also see: Death of a Parent; Natural Disasters; Protection against Sexual Abuse]

FOSTER CARE

C HILDREN MAY live away from their biological parents for various reasons and lengths of time when biological parents are unable to provide care for their children. This is called *foster care*.

What Children Might Experience Depends On:

- The age of the child when placed. A newborn may become more attached to the substitute caregiver than the biological parent.
- The reason for the placement.
- How long the placement lasts.
- Whether there is ongoing contact with the biological parents and the quality of this contact.
- The relationship with the substitute caregivers prior to placement. Did the child know and love the new caregivers prior to living with them?
- The number of previous placements the child has experienced.
- Whether the child's questions about out-of-home care have been answered honestly and clearly. This allows the child to understand why his parents are not able to take care of him.
- Whether the child's grief at the loss of his parents is respected and validated.
- The quality of emotional warmth, security, love, and one-to-one attention the child receives in the placement.
- Whether the child is given a spiritual framework to interpret

the experience. Children should be told that God understands that this is a hard time and will help them.

- The unique personality of the child. Other siblings who are placed in foster care at the same time will respond in ways that are unique to their own personalities.

What Parents Can Do:

Regardless of the circumstances of the placement away from the biological parents, the child will maintain attachment to the biological parents. A child forced to choose loyalty to foster parents over biological parents will usually choose her biological parents. Children feel supported when they understand that their biological parents may love them and yet not be able to provide day-to-day care for them.

If the biological parents do not demonstrate love or interest in the child, the child can be told that he is a lovable child and that there is nothing about him that caused his parents to be unable to care for him. Children may assume that they are rejected due to some quality in themselves that makes it impossible for the parents to provide care.

Life in substitute care is usually quite different from life with biological parents. Children need time to learn new expectations and routines. Children often assume that new caregivers accept them only when they show good behavior. Many children initially will "honeymoon" (act very good) until they feel safe enough to show their real feelings.

Children need help with how to answer questions from outsiders about why they are living in substitute care. They can be told that they do not owe a thorough explanation to everyone who asks. The child can say, "I am living with this family because my mom and dad aren't able to take care of me just now."

▶ WHAT THE BIBLE SAYS:

Isaiah 43:4-5   You are precious to me. I give you honor, and I love you. . . . So don't be afraid. I am with you.

Isaiah 61:2   He has sent me to comfort all those who are sad.

2 Thessalonians 3:16   We pray that the Lord of peace will give you peace at all times and in every way. May the Lord be with all of you.

▶ WHAT TO SAY:

"Your mom and dad can learn to take care of you. I don't think anyone ever showed them how to take care of kids."

"I know that you miss your mom. It's okay to love both of us."

"When you feel sad about missing your parents, you can tell me. Any kid would feel bad. That's a normal feeling."

"God knows where you are every minute. He loves your mom and dad, and he loves you."

"There is nothing about the kind of kid you are that made your mom and dad unable to take care of you."

"It's okay to talk about the hard stuff that happened when you were living at home. I won't be mad at you or at your folks."

"You can call us Mom and Dad if you want to. We know that we are just your mom and dad for now."

"Hitting others is not okay in this house. When you are mad you can put it into words, hit the punching bag, or take time out. You can learn to think before you act."

"Here is a picture album of your time in our home. We will never forget you and we will always want the best for you."

"Your dad made some wrong decisions. You can make good choices."

"I'm glad you told your school counselor about your problems at home. You were smart and brave to ask for help."

[Also see: Fears and Worries]

MURDER

CHILDREN WHO have "witnessed" thousands of murders on television have little knowledge about the reality of suffering a victim's family and friends experience. Children may attend a church with a prison ministry, but rarely will children be exposed to a victims ministry. Children can learn about the unique needs of these families and pray for them.

When children read newspaper articles about murder, it is helpful to talk about the probable emotions of the family of the victim. Since violence is increasing, many children will know someone who was murdered. These children can be taught specific ways to demonstrate practical love.

What to Tell Children:

- It is a myth that sorrow draws a family closer together. The truth is that a murder puts great stress on family relationships.

- Families believe that they will feel better when the trial is over and the murderer goes to prison, but usually the painful feelings continue. Punishing the murderer doesn't help as much as they thought it would.

- It takes much longer for families to grieve a murder than to grieve an expected death from an illness.

- Telling a family member that they have to put this behind them and get on with their life isn't helpful and will make grieving families angry.

Children Who Experience a Murder in the Family May Wonder:

- Why God didn't protect the person who was murdered. Parents can tell children that we live in a world where bad things can happen to anyone.
- Why the police can't find the murderer and punish him.
- Why a murderer is out on parole in a short time.
- Why justice sometimes depends on whether you have the best lawyer.
- Why bad things are said about the victim in the courtroom. Parents should give brief, simple, factual information.

What Parents Need to Know:

- Children sometimes see inaccurate news stories on TV or in the newspaper about the murder. Sometimes the victim is blamed for being murdered; for example, someone might say, "They shouldn't have been in that part of town." Remind children that no one wants to be murdered.
- Parents often divorce after the murder of a child, so surviving children may grieve both the murder and the divorce.
- Emotions are often volatile after a murder, and children are frightened by the intense anger in the home.
- Parents may be preoccupied with the events of the murder and unable to support the surviving children.
- Young children believe that life is fair, that the good guy wins and the bad guy is punished. A murder in the family may shatter this fantasy.
- Parents may be overprotective of the remaining children. This causes children to feel unsafe.
- It takes many years for a family to heal after a murder, so children may experience most of their growing-up years in a family that is focused on the murder.

▶ WHAT THE BIBLE SAYS:

Exodus 20:13 "You must not murder anyone."

Matthew 5:21 "You have heard that it was said to our people long ago, 'You must not murder anyone. Anyone who murders another will be judged.'"

▶ WHAT TO SAY:

"You are an important helper and can invite your friend over to play whenever you want. He needs time away from the tension at home."

"They are angry because of the murder. You are not the cause of the bad feelings."

"This is what will happen in the courtroom . . ."

"I know you feel mad enough to want to hurt the murderer yourself. He is responsible to God for what he did."

"When you feel angry you can hit this pillow, or dig in the yard, or play softball."

"You couldn't have protected her from being murdered. None of us could have stopped it."

"Of course you can write a letter to the family and tell about some of your happy memories of the person who died."

"One way we can help is by being practical. Would you like to help me weed their flower beds on Saturday?"

"It is okay to have fun and to laugh with your friend. It doesn't mean he doesn't feel bad about the murder."

"You can help your friend with her schoolwork. I think she must have a hard time concentrating since the murder."

"It must be hard to believe that the police don't care."

"Your mom and I can support the family by going to the trial and by listening to their feelings afterward."

[Also see: Capital Punishment; Death of a Parent; Gangs]

SELF-ESTEEM

THE NUMBER one job in the emotional care of children is helping them develop a healthy self-concept, a balance of confidence and humility.

How Self-esteem Becomes Damaged:

- Children dislike themselves in direct relationship to the amount of rejection and criticism they experience. Children believe the assessment of adults.

- Children who have been pushed beyond their capabilities will always fail.

- Comparisons of one child to another always leaves one child the loser.

- Children may feel loved but not respected in the family. Children need both love and respect to feel good about themselves.

- Children are constantly compared with other children at school.

- Children are repeatedly exposed to non-Christian values in assessing their self-worth, including physical beauty, intelligence, athletic skill, musical talent, or wealth.

- Children have no way to determine the value of another person's opinion of their worth. They believe that if a grown-up said it, it must be true.

- Children who have been overprotected by their parents may be unprepared for the real world.

Building Healthy Self-esteem in Children:

- Feeling dumb can be an excuse not to try. Give children one simple confidence-building step at a time.
- Talking with a child about his worth is a beginning, but it will have to be repeated again and again in many settings.
- Asking a child her opinion and then following her request tells the child her opinion matters.
- Spending one-to-one time with a child says he is important. Focused attention is more affirming than general attention.
- Tell children that working hard and making friends are more important abilities than being pretty or talented.
- Teach children how to fail. Be casual about failure. It is the only way to learn something new.
- A child needs successes. Teach her to be an expert at doing something.
- Refer to the child's strengths in matter-of-fact conversation with others in the child's presence.
- Tell the child about your own past failures, not just your successes, especially in areas where the child has more skill than you did at his age.
- Don't allow children to blame someone else for their failures.

▶ WHAT THE BIBLE SAYS:

1 Samuel 16:7   God does not see the same way people see. People look at the outside of a person, but the Lord looks at the heart.

Ephesians 3:12   In Christ we can come before God with freedom and without fear.

Ephesians 3:20   With God's power working in us, God can do much, much more than anything we can ask or think of.

1 Timothy 4:12   You are young, but do not let anyone treat you as if you were not important.

▶ WHAT TO SAY:

"I like the way you did your homework today without being reminded. I think you are more responsible than I was at your age."

"You are good at fishing. Most of the boys in your class don't know as much about fishing as you do."

"I know that you would rather play than finish cleaning your room, but in our family we work hard, then we are free to play."

"God made you special. There will never be another person in all of human history just like you."

"Yes, learning is hard work, but you can do it if you keep at it."

"When people tease you, you can walk away from them. Others are not the boss of how you feel."

"Today was your spelling test. I was thinking about you and praying for you. How did it go?"

"You are so much fun to be with."

"I like to watch the way you help Grandma. You are a kind person."

"I think you made a good decision."

"God knew how much we would love having you in the family."

"I can see that you put a lot of work into making this. I like the way you stick to a job until you finish it."

"You are going to be a wonderful dad someday."

"Yes, you lost the race, but you improved your time, and that is what is important."

"God's love for you is not based on how smart you are, how good you are, or how you look."

"Your mom and I are so glad we get to be your parents."

[Also see: Fears and Worries; How to Make Friends]

SUICIDE

CHILDREN CAN be told that *suicide* is deciding to die and then acting on it by doing something to cause death. In addition, children can be told that persons who attempt suicide may not know that there is help available for them and that there are other and better solutions to their problems.

What Parents Need to Know:

There are a variety of reasons why a person might consider suicide, including:

- Feeling very sad and hopeless
- Being mentally ill
- Experiencing a great loss
- Not knowing how to solve problems
- Not having supportive friends
- Having a serious illness

But, in all of these circumstances there is help and hope. There is never a circumstance in which suicide is the real answer to a problem.

Old people, middle-aged people, teenagers, and children attempt suicide. Some of the clues that a young person might be thinking about suicide are:

- A big change in personality, either very sad or happy
- Giving away prized possessions

- Telling friends good-bye
- Not paying attention at school and getting bad grades
- Performing dangerous activities that might result in being hurt, such as playing with guns or cutting their skin
- Not wanting to be with friends; sleeping or watching TV too much
- Talking about death or listening to music about death
- Making negative remarks about themselves, such as, "I'm not good at anything"
- Using drugs or alcohol
- Feeling very angry or rebellious
- Recently breaking up with a special friend
- Saying that they feel hopeless

What Children Might Experience:

Some children know someone who has attempted suicide. If this person was a parent, children may think that suicide is inherited. They need to be told that it isn't, but a parent's example of suicide may lead children to think that suicide is the way to deal with difficult problems. Caring adults can teach children to eliminate suicide as an option and to consider other, better choices. When children believe that suicide is a solution to a difficult but temporary problem, they must be told that to commit suicide is to be dead forever.

Children who have a parent who has committed suicide may grow up with a sense of guilt, anger, and worthlessness. They must be told that no one causes another person to commit suicide.

Sometimes children and teenagers make suicide attempts as a way to let grown-ups know how much they are hurting inside. A suicide attempt should be taken very seriously even if it is not the kind of attempt that could kill a person.

Children should be told the truth when someone they know commits suicide. Families may develop a myth about why the person died because it is hard to believe that a family member chose to die. Children can be told that most people who attempt suicide have mixed feelings about wanting to be dead, and that usually they just don't want to hurt anymore.

▶ WHAT THE BIBLE SAYS:

Psalm 91:1-2   Those who go to God Most High for safety will be protected by God All-Powerful. I will say to the Lord, "You are my place of safety and protection. You are my God, and I trust you."

1 Corinthians 6:19-20   You should know that your body is a temple for the Holy Spirit. The Holy Spirit is in you. You have received the Holy Spirit from God. You do not own yourselves. You were bought by God for a price. So honor God with your bodies.

Galatians 3:29   You belong to Christ.

▶ WHAT TO SAY:

"I asked my friend if he was feeling so bad that he might hurt himself. I knew I couldn't talk anybody into committing suicide by asking if he had thought about it."

"You can ask your friend to promise that she won't hurt herself."

"I'm glad that you told me what your friend said. No one should keep that information a secret."

"You could invite your depressed friend to help you take care of our neighbor's dog. Directing her attention toward others might help."

"Drinking alcohol will only make him more depressed."

"Your friend sounds very sad. How about going with him to talk to the school counselor?"

"I know that you promised you wouldn't tell anyone what he said. You can tell him that it is not a promise you can keep."

"It helps to ask how a person is feeling, and then listen well."

"Do you know about the suicide hot line? Let me show you how to find the phone number in the book."

"A person who feels like committing suicide needs the help of a counselor or doctor, but he also needs friends."

"I know the family did not understand that he was thinking about suicide. They would have helped if they had known."

"We won't try to get them to admit it was a suicide. It is too hard for some people to acknowledge at first."

"Of course we will go over to visit the family. Since the suicide, they need our help more than ever."

[Also see: Euthanasia; Funerals; War]

DEATH OF A PET

FOR MANY children the death of a loved pet is their first major experience with grief. Children grieve as deeply over the death of a pet as an adult might for the death of a loved friend. The grief shouldn't be minimized. As much as parents would like to protect children from pain, loss is an inevitable part of childhood. It can be a time of growth for children and help prepare them for future losses.

Children respond uniquely to the death of a pet depending on how old the child is, how much they loved the pet, and whether they knew the pet might die. Some children are angry; some withdraw. Some children will talk about it. Others won't.

How Parents Can Support Children:

- Allow the child to place pictures of the pet on a bulletin board or in a scrapbook. Encourage remembering.
- Help the child have a Good-bye Ceremony. This might include holding hands and thanking God for such a special pet and telling God how sad the child feels.
- A small pet can be buried in the backyard with flowers placed on the grave. The ceremony can close with everyone saying one nice thing about the pet.
- It is okay for parents to cry in front of children.
- Don't use the pet's name again for a new pet.
- Give children warning if a pet's death is expected.
- Tell the child the truth when he asks questions. To the ques-

tion, "Will Fluffy be in heaven?" you can say, "God doesn't tell us, but he DOES say we will have everything we need in heaven to be happy."

- Children may grieve for months. Usually the grief will surface with new reminders of his pet's death. Don't attempt to distract the child from the pain. To love is to grieve.

- It is okay for a child to see the pet's body after it has died.

- Children can be told that the pet doesn't hurt when it is dead and that death is final.

- Don't replace the pet immediately with a new pet. Give the child time to mourn. A new pet can never replace a pet that has died.

▶ WHAT THE BIBLE SAYS:

Psalm 147:3 He heals the brokenhearted. He bandages their wounds.

Proverbs 12:10 A good man takes care of his animals.

1 Peter 5:7 Give all your worries to him, because he cares for you.

▶ WHAT TO SAY:

"I feel really sad too."

"It's okay to play. It doesn't mean you're not sad about his death."

"I know that she was a very special friend to you."

"Any child would feel sad to lose a loved pet."

"You can ask me any questions you like. If I don't know the answer, I will tell you."

"You did such a good job of taking care of your pet."

"It is okay to cry and it is okay not to cry. Everyone feels sad in the way that is right for him."

"What do you miss the most since Fluffy died?"

"Someday you may want another pet, but I know that a new pet won't replace this one."

"What do you wonder about?"

"It takes awhile for the sad feelings to leave. Nobody expects you to get over this right away."

[Also see: Euthanasia]

Religious
Topics

CREATION VS. EVOLUTION

 OUNG CHILDREN in public schools may be taught by trusted teachers that evolution is scientific fact, not theory.

What to Tell Children:

- Evolutionary theory is a belief system and cannot be proven, just as Christian faith in a Creator God is a belief system which cannot be scientifically proven. Both are a matter of faith.

- There has never been any discovery in science that has disproved the biblical account of creation. True science and Scripture never disagree.

- God created Adam as a fully grown man. Human beings didn't begin as monkeys that gradually, over millions of years, turned into human beings.

- There is no evidence that there are any missing links. One species does not become another species; fish don't become frogs, birds don't become lizards, monkeys don't become people.

- Charles Darwin, the founder of the evolution theory, admitted that there weren't any true examples of a species that were half animal and half human. There still aren't.

- To believe in evolution, a person must deny known scientific truth. For example, nature moves from order to chaos, not from chaos to order, which would be necessary for evolution. Things run down, get old, die, or decay. They don't improve.

- It takes more faith to believe in evolution than to believe in the biblical account of creation! It is mathematically impossible that intelligent life came by chance.
- God created everything out of absolutely nothing. The world did not begin with a big bang; even a big bang must result from something.
- The only One that has never been created is God. He didn't have a beginning. He was always God.
- The tiny complicated details of the world make it hard to imagine that it somehow just happened without an intelligent Creator.
- The word *evolution* may be used to mean change, such as a child turning (or evolving) into a teenager. That is not the same thing as saying a dog turns into a cat.

Teaching Children How to Respond to Teaching about Evolution:

- Children can be told that it is wrong to be disrespectful to teachers who present the theory of evolution.
- Children can state that they know that evolution has not been proven to be true, and that they believe it is more logical to believe that God created the world than to believe that it somehow came together by chance.
- Children can write reports or give talks about the option of belief in creation by God.
- Children may choose not to confront peers or teachers in the classroom, but can talk about the creation-evolution debate in the safety of home or Sunday school.

▶ WHAT THE BIBLE SAYS:

Genesis 1:1   In the beginning God created the sky and the earth.

Genesis 1:27   So God created human beings in his image. In the image of God he created them. He created them male and female.

▶ WHAT TO SAY:

"Since God made us, that means we are responsible to him."

"God made all people in his own image, and that is why we respect others."

"When someone believes something that isn't true, I pray and ask God to help me talk to them about what the Bible says."

"The Bible doesn't tell us very much about how God created the earth, only that he did create it."

"Since God created the world to function like it does, there will never be scientific facts that disagree with what the Bible says."

"Let's thank God for making such a beautiful world!"

"God must have a good sense of humor to make a giraffe, a hippopotamus, and a monkey."

"It is amazing that a tiny fetus grows inside a mother's uterus into a baby ready to be born. Can you imagine that just happening?"

"I think it is hard for people to admit that evolution is not true, because if they do, they would have to admit that God is in charge, not human beings!"

"There are many very smart scientists who know that God created the heavens and the earth."

"I brought home a video about bees. Let's look at it together tonight and remember that God made bees and built into them the ability to make honey."

"In the beginning God created the earth, and when he is ready, he will stop human life on the earth. Then we will go to heaven."

[Also see: How Do I Know There Really Is a God?]

Do Good People Really Go to Hell?

What to Tell Children:

ANSWERING THE question, "Do good people really go to hell?" clearly helps children understand the basic teaching of the Bible. At the same time, the question must be answered with humility. We do not always know the relationship another person has with God. Specifically, the most common questions are:

What about people who don't accept Jesus?

Once children clearly understand that becoming a Christian means that they will live forever in heaven, it is logical that they will ask what happens to people who do not accept Christ. It is easier, of course, to talk about this concept in general terms than to address it following the death of a loved non-Christian relative.

What about people who have never even heard about Jesus?

In addition, children may ask if people who have never heard about Jesus will go to hell, such as people in foreign countries who have never had the teaching of a missionary.

Isn't being a good person all that is necessary?

It is confusing for children to consider that being good is not the criteria for going to heaven, since good behavior is commonly associated with rewards for the child. Children may also believe that people who are born into a Christian family, go to church regularly, are baptized, take communion, or obey the golden rule will go to heaven when they die.

The Bible Teaches:

- Everybody is a sinner.
- Sin separates us from God.
- God sent Jesus to die for our sin.
- We have to accept God's gift of salvation.
- It isn't possible to be good enough to go to heaven. Even if they did the best they could every single day, they still would not be perfect, and perfection is what God requires in order to live with him in heaven.
- Tell the child that Jesus said that we were to "Love the Lord your God with all your heart, soul and mind." And, in addition, to "love your neighbor as you love yourself" (Matt. 22:37-39). Children can understand that neither they, nor anyone they know, has been able to do that perfectly.
- People measure good differently than God measures good. For a child to be good means that he is better than his friends, or at least no worse than them. But God is clear that the only way to heaven is to accept Christ because he is the only one who is good enough to be acceptable to God.
- God never forces anyone to accept him, and a person who chooses to live without God in this world will live without God in the next world.
- The Bible teaches that everyone has the chance to respond to God, even people who have never heard about Jesus. God shows who he is through nature and by putting a desire to know the true God in the heart of every person born. God doesn't want anyone to choose to go to hell, so everyone has

the chance to believe in God, even people who have never read the Bible.

- Being sincere in your beliefs is not enough to be accepted by Christ because people can be sincerely wrong. A person may not believe that a gun is loaded, but he still will kill someone if he shoots the gun, and he was wrong.

- The Bible teaches that children who are too little to understand how to accept Christ will go to heaven.

God doesn't send good people to hell. God simply carried out the decision of the person to accept or reject him. We decide whether we will go to heaven or hell, not God. The Bible says that "all people have sinned and are not good enough for God's glory" (Rom. 3:23). Even people who are very, very good won't go to heaven unless they accept God's free gift of salvation. "He who believes in God's Son is not judged guilty" (John 3:18). God made a way so that no one has to go to hell.

▶ WHAT THE BIBLE SAYS:

John 3:5 But Jesus answered, "I tell you the truth. Unless one is born from water and the Spirit, he cannot enter God's kingdom."

John 3:16-17 For God loved the world so much that he gave his only Son. God gave his Son so that whoever believes in him may not be lost, but have eternal life. God did not send his Son into the world to judge the world guilty, but to save the world through him.

▶ WHAT TO SAY:

"God loves everyone in the whole world and wants everyone to live in heaven with him."

"It is easier for people to choose to invite Jesus into their hearts if we tell them what the Bible says about going to heaven."

"You and Daddy and I will live in heaven with God after we die because we have asked God to forgive our sins and we've asked him to be the boss of our lives."

"One of the reasons we give money at church for the missionaries is so they can teach people in other countries what God said in the Bible."

"Heaven is a wonderful place. Would you like me to read some of the Bible verses that describe it?"

"Jesus died so no one would have to go to hell."

"Sometimes we don't know if a person has invited Jesus into their heart, but God knows."

[Also see: New Age; Which Church Is Right?]

HALLOWEEN

What Parents Need to Know:

CHRISTIAN PARENTS may have mixed feelings about celebrating a holiday that focuses on goblins, ghosts, and witches. Some Christians believe that participating in Halloween events is a form of honoring Satan, and that it is wrong to allow children to dress in devil costumes to try to scare others while trick-or-treating. They point to the history of the holiday as a celebration of the ancient Celtic New Year and the transition from the light of summer to the darkness of winter. Great bonfires were lit to the Lord of Death, also known as the Grim Reaper, leader of ghosts. The Celts also thought that on October 31 the souls of dead people and all the witches, demons, and evil spirits were allowed to roam the earth. They believed that cats were sacred because they had been human beings once and were turned into cats as punishment for evil deeds. The Irish believed that a man named Jack was not permitted passage into heaven because he played tricks on the devil, so he was forced to walk the earth with his lantern until judgment day.

Halloween is also historically celebrated as All Hallows' Eve, or evening of the saints. It is a day observed by some Christians as a time to remember the holy ones who have died and whose names are known only to God.

No matter what way parents decide that Halloween is to be observed, children should understand why there are differences of opinion about the celebration of this day. This way, they can be sensitive to others.

What Parents Can Do:

Why Children Like Halloween:

- They get candy, dress in interesting costumes, and attend parties.
- It allows children to challenge their fears of the dark, ghosts, and witches in a safe setting. It is fun for children to be scared, but not too scared. They enjoy the opportunity to laugh at pretend monsters who turn out to be playmates.
- Children deal with their fears by identifying with the feared person or thing. Becoming the scary monster, instead of the victim of the monster, makes children feel powerful, instead of weak.

Young children who cannot separate reality from make-believe need to be protected from excessive fear at Halloween. Adolescents need direction regarding acceptable videos and movies. Blood-and-gore films that contain graphic murder scenes are not appropriate. Parties which have seances, Ouija boards, or fortune-tellers are inappropriate. Vandalism is not appropriate. Killing small animals is not appropriate.

Suggestions for Halloween Night:

- Have costume parties where kids come dressed as a Bible character (not Satan!).
- Have Bible houses, instead of haunted houses, where children can see different Bible stories acted out.
- Give tracts with treats.
- Have a harvest party in a barn with rowdy games, apple bobbing, and square dancing.
- For teens, gather around a bonfire at the beach or in the woods to listen to animated readings from *Foxe's Book of Martyrs*.

▶ WHAT THE BIBLE SAYS:

Luke 10:19-20 I gave you more power than the Enemy has.

Nothing will hurt you. You should be happy, but not because the spirits obey you. You should be happy because your names are written in heaven.

▶ WHAT TO SAY:

"God made every day, including October 31. It isn't Satan's day. It's God's day."

"God's direction for how we are to live doesn't change on Halloween. We still need to be kind and sensitive to others."

"We don't need to be afraid of witches and ghosts. God is more powerful than Satan."

"It's fun to dress up and play make-believe. I'm glad that you know it is only pretend."

"You can eat all the candy you want tonight, and then we will throw the rest away. Candy is yummy but will hurt your teeth if you eat it every day."

"If you are frightened, please tell me. You are safe with me."

"Your dad will go with you trick-or-treating. Most adults are safe, but some are not."

"I'm glad that you are going trick-or-treating with your friends. It is best to go in a group."

"Don't eat any of the candy until you get home. Then we can check what is safe for you to eat."

"Some Christians don't believe in celebrating Halloween because ..."

"Some kids dress up like the devil to go trick-or-treating, but the real devil is not cute or easy to recognize."

"If you go to a Halloween party and are asked to participate in activities that are wrong, such as vandalizing someone's property, you can find a phone and call home. We'll come and pick you up."

[Also see: Occult]

How Do I Know There Really Is A God?

VERY YOUNG children find it easy to accept the reality of God. It is not until children reach grade-school years that questions about proving the existence of God may occur to them. Children can be told that God left evidence of his existence and that it makes more sense to accept that God is real than to deny that there is a God. Believing in God is logical.

How We Know That God Exists:

- God said that he exists and he told us about himself in the Bible. If the Bible is true, then God exists.

- God sent Jesus Christ to show us what God is like. Whatever is true about Jesus is true about God. Jesus said that he and God were the same person.

- When Jesus came back to life after being dead, he proved that he was God. No one but God could do that.

- Many smart, thinking people believe that God exists.

- We know God is real because people are born with the desire to know God.

- To imagine our complicated world just happening without a

Creator is as ridiculous as thinking that a box of one thousand puzzle pieces could put themselves together inside a box, without any help.

- People have a strong sense of right and wrong. This came from God. If there is no God, then where did we get our sense of right and wrong?
- When people accept that God is real and begin a relationship with him, their lives change. God changes people.
- Since Jesus told lots of people he is God, a person must either accept that it is true or believe that Jesus was a terrible liar.
- If there is no God, then why do people exist? What would be the purpose of life?

Children can be told that the existence of God cannot be proved in the same way a scientific experiment is proved. It is a reasonable belief, and there is much evidence to support belief in God, but the bottom line is that it requires faith to accept the reality of God, just as it requires faith to deny the reality of God.

Why Can't We See God?

Children may ask why they can't see God since he is real. They can be told that God doesn't have a body now, like he did when Jesus was on earth. God is a Spirit. It is like the wind, which they can't see, but they can see what wind does, or like love, which they can't see, but they know is real.

Children can be told that one of the names of God is Emmanuel, which means that "God is with us." Whether we can see him or not, he is always with us.

Is There One God, or Are There Many Gods?

There is only one God. Some people believe there are many gods, but that doesn't make it true.

▶ WHAT THE BIBLE SAYS:

Romans 1:20 There are things about God that people cannot see—his eternal power and all the things that make him God. But since the beginning of the world those things have been easy to understand. They are made clear by what God has made. So people have no excuse for the bad things they do.

1 John 5:9-12   We believe people when they say something is true. But what God says is more important. And he has told us the truth about his own Son. Anyone who believes in the Son of God has the truth that God told us. Anyone who does not believe makes God a liar. He does not believe what God told us about his Son. This is what God told us: God has given us eternal life, and this life is in his Son. Whoever has the Son has life. But the person who does not have the Son of God does not have life.

▶ WHAT TO SAY:

"God is real and wants people to have a friendship with him."

"It doesn't help to argue with someone who doesn't believe in God. It will only make him angry. Just tell him why you believe in God."

"Live so your friends know that you have invited Jesus to come into your heart and that he is helping you live for him."

"It takes more faith to believe that there isn't a God, than to believe there is a God."

"You can feel strong and sure about your belief. The Bible says that someday everyone in the whole world will know that Jesus is God."

"God made a beautiful world for us, didn't he?"

"Daddy and I are going to pray about that and ask God to help our family make the right choice."

"Have you noticed how Mr. Jones is changing since he invited God to come into his life?"

"I don't actually hear God's voice, but God lets me know what he wants me to do by putting good ideas into my head, and by the advice he gives through other Christians, and by what the Bible says. That's the way God talks to me."

[Also see: Creation vs. Evolution; Which Church Is Right?]

OCCULT

What Parents Need to Know:

Children at risk for occult involvement:

CHILDREN AT risk during adolescence often come from Christian families because these children are accustomed to a spiritual framework for explaining the events of life. They may come from any social or economic status but are most likely to come from suburban, middle-class families. They may be children who:

- Use drugs or alcohol
- Have divorced parents
- Are fascinated with evil and attracted to the mysterious
- Have above average intelligence
- Feel alienated from mainstream peers and "the system"
- Have a strong need to control
- Are highly creative

Identification with the occult allows and encourages adolescent rebellion and defiance and fosters feeling special. Children who have been abused are at great risk for occult involvement. Occult affiliation is attractive to these adolescents because it offers them a sense of belonging to a close community; permission to have sex without guilt; power and excitement. In addition, many children become involved in occult activities because they are curious.

How do I know if my child is getting involved in the occult?

Approximately 30 to 40 percent of high school students have some involvement in the occult before finishing high school. Common early behavior includes:

- Using Ouija boards at parties
- Listening obsessively to black metal (satanic) music
- Wearing satanic jewelry (such as inverted pentagrams)
- Collecting chalices, skulls, black candles
- Dying hair black, painting one or two fingernails black
- Wearing all black clothing or T-shirts decorated with demons
- Lying about where they are going
- Losing interest in schoolwork, declining grades
- Preferring movies and books about horror and violence
- Doodling pentagrams, skulls, death themes
- Growing disrespect for parents and siblings
- Resisting church attendance
- Increasing use of swearing and obscenity
- Suffering from depression
- Writing in a "Book of Shadows" (a journal of quotes from a satanic bible, backward language, and lyrics promoting suicide)
- Not bringing friends home to meet parents
- Being preoccupied with Dungeons and Dragons game
- Declaring bedroom off-limits to parents

What Parents Can Do:

- Children want loving authority in the home. They feel secure when adults have clear guidelines. Occult groups expect submission to the control of the leader. When there is an authority vacuum at home, children seek direction outside the home.

- Children want to belong and feel emotionally close in a family. The child who finds comfort, support, and encouragement in his family will have little need to seek it elsewhere.

    1. Close families enjoy playing together.
    2. Children in close families are accustomed to hearing parents ask for the forgiveness of their children when they have wronged them.
    3. Both children and parents feel honored and respected in their differences and unique gifts.
    4. Children in close families know that no matter what they do, they will always be loved.

- Even very young children need a spiritual framework for life and a commitment to a cause that makes demands of them as well as offers acceptance and forgiveness.

- Children need to learn to rely on the authority of Scripture, rather than on their feelings. The occult appeals to certain emotional needs.

- Set clear limits. There is no reason a child should read a satanic bible.

- Ask other Christian adults to pray for your child.

- Tell the child that you cannot allow anything in your home that has satanic significance (jewelry, T-shirts, candles, or skulls, for example), then remove such items.

- Play Christian music in your home.

- Help kids build friendships with Christian teens by hosting parties or planning outings such as fishing trips.

- Listen, love, understand, laugh. Make home a wonderful place to be.

▶ WHAT THE BIBLE SAYS:

Leviticus 19:31 Do not go to mediums or fortune-tellers for advice. If you do, you will become unclean. I am the Lord your God.

Ephesians 6:11-13 Wear the full armor of God. Wear God's armor so that you can fight against the devil's evil tricks. Our fight is not against people on earth. We are fighting against the rulers and authorities and the powers of this world's darkness.

We are fighting against the spiritual powers of evil in the heavenly world. That is why you need to get God's full armor.

▶ WHAT TO SAY:

"The way you know whether a belief is right or not is whether it is consistent with what the Bible teaches."

"Your cousin Jim is wearing occult T-shirts. We are going to pray for him, and love him, and invite him over to our house often. He needs to know we care about him."

"Would you like to learn about what the occult teaches?"

"Feeling good about something is not the same as being right about it."

"The Bible teaches that Satan likes to pretend that he is someone that he isn't or that certain behaviors aren't dangerous, when they really are. Satan is a liar."

"Some kids get involved in the occult before they really know the harm. Curiosity can be dangerous."

"We don't read horoscopes in this family because God is the only one who knows the future, and we can trust him with whatever happens."

"When you memorize Bible verses, it makes Satan really mad. He knows how powerful God's Word is."

"Jesus believed in a real Satan."

"You need to know about Satan, but you don't need to be afraid of him."

[Also see: Halloween; New Age; Which Church Is Right?]

SANTA CLAUS

What Parents Need to Know:

MOST CHRISTIAN parents and their children support and enjoy the temporary myths of Santa Claus, the Easter Bunny, and the Tooth Fairy. They do not experience these to be in conflict with Christian faith.

A vivid imagination is a normal part of childhood and adds wonder and excitement in addition to encouraging creative thinking in young children. It does not, as may be feared, create distrust in children for what their parents tell them.

In Christian homes, the emphasis during the holiday season will be on the story of the birth of Christ. Children can be taken to local maternity wards to look into the newborn nursery windows to help them understand how tiny Jesus was. They can make gifts and leave them on the doorsteps of people who need a surprise. They can play with a crèche scene to reenact the Christmas story. These activities will diminish the focus on Santa as the central character of Christmas.

Believing in Santa is simply an extension of "let's pretend." It does not make it more difficult for children to distinguish between fact and fantasy. Trust in parents is based on more significant issues than the story of Santa Claus.

What Parents Can Do:

At some point, children want to know if Santa is real. They

can be told that Santa is a make-believe person and that it is fun to believe that he brings presents that are actually given by parents. Children delight in knowing that their parents have enjoyed playing this game with them. When there are younger siblings in the family, older children who know the truth enjoy feeling like insiders by aligning with their parents in keeping the story alive until these brothers and sisters are also ready to let go of the fantasy. Normally there is a transition period in which children become suspicious and begin to let go of belief in Santa. Questions such as, "How come there are so many different Santas in stores?" or "I saw a Santa suit in Grandpa's closet" or "How can Santa get into our house when we don't have a chimney?" indicate that the child is ready to know the truth. Parents can maintain a playful attitude in talking about Santa, and the child will sense that Santa may not be real.

This weaning from belief in Santa Claus often occurs sometime between four and eight years of age. At four, the majority of children still believe in Santa, but by eight, only a small percentage retain a serious belief that Santa is real. In the meantime, children enjoy thinking that there is a magical character in the world who enjoys giving them special gifts, just as many adults enjoy imagining how they would spend the winnings of a sweepstakes.

What to Tell Children:

Once a child is ready to give up belief in Santa, parents should not avoid disclosing the truth even though it is hard for parents to see their child growing up. When children know there is not a real Santa and parents persist in trying to convince the child that Santa Claus is real, trust in parents may be damaged.

Children can be told that the joy, the magic, and the spirit of giving are all very *real* and that Santa represents these qualities. Children should be told that other Christian families may object to belief in the myth of Santa, and that is a choice that parents make. Reassure children that the account of Jesus' birth as written in the Bible really happened. It is not like pretending there is a Santa. They can be reminded that Jesus is the One who came to give us the best gifts of love, forgiveness, salvation, and life forever with him in heaven. That is far better than anything Santa could provide!

▶ WHAT THE BIBLE SAYS:

Luke 2:11   Today your Savior was born in David's town. He is Christ, the Lord.

1 Timothy 1:4   Tell them not to spend their time on stories that are not true.

▶ WHAT TO SAY:

"What do you think about Santa?"

"It's been fun to pretend with you that Santa is a real person."

"Children in other countries have different beliefs about Santa Claus."

"If you ever wonder if something is really true, I will always tell you."

"When I was little I thought Santa was . . . "

"I'm so glad that Jesus is real and that all of the stories in the Bible actually happened."

"Even if you know that Santa is just a pretend person, it is still fun to watch the Christmas videos about Santa and smile."

"When did you first start figuring this out?"

"When you were sound asleep, Mommy and I would get all the presents we had wrapped and hidden away and put them under the tree, and then eat the cookies and milk you left for Santa. It was so much fun to see your face in the morning!"

THE NEW AGE

CHILDREN ARE exposed to New Age ideas in subtle ways. Because the language of the New Age may sound compatible with Christian belief, many children have difficulty understanding that the New Age movement is in conflict with Christian faith. Parents, fearful of the influence of the New Age, may remove children from public school classrooms to home school or Christian schools, but children will still be exposed to New Age ideas through cartoons, toys, comic books, video games, library books, and movies. In addition, Christian adults have a responsibility to change the public school environment for the protection of other children, even when their own children are removed from these schools.

What Parents Need to Know:

New Age Teachings vs. Christian Teachings:

- New Age teaches that Jesus was a good man and teacher, but not the only true God. New Age believes that we can learn from all of the world's religions, even satanism. There is acceptance for Christian belief as long as people value all other faiths as equal to Christian faith.

- New Age teaches that people can get to heaven without the death and resurrection of Jesus Christ.

- New Age believes that man is a god and emphasizes human potential and man's ability to become anything he wants to be.

- New Age teaches that lessons not learned in this lifetime will be learned by returning to earth in another form by reincarnation. A Gallup poll revealed that one in four Americans now believe in reincarnation.

- New Age followers believe that each person decides what is right for him or her. There is no ultimate standard. That's not what the Bible teaches.

- Christians believe in the virgin birth, sin, Satan and hell, and that the God of the Bible is the only true God. These are all unacceptable beliefs to followers of the New Age.

- Many New Age followers are involved in practices such as belief in the power of crystals, pyramids, channeling, Ouija boards, crystal balls, talking with the dead, past lives, horoscopes, and astrology. These are practices that are condemned in the Bible.

- New Age places more focus on feeling good than being right.

What Children Might Experience:

Children may be confused by the toleration and acceptance of New Age followers who accept Christian belief as another option. Children can be told that the Bible is the only true standard.

In addition, children may be confused by many of the good ideas of the New Age, such as the practice is good, but the reason for the practice is wrong. For example:

NEW AGE:	CHRISTIANITY:
CLEAN UP THE ENVIRONMENT because everything is god and god is everything.	CLEAN UP THE ENVIRONMENT because God the Creator gave us the responsibility to care for his world.
ACCEPT EACH OTHER because whatever a person believes is okay.	ACCEPT EACH OTHER because God loves all people and died for them.

NEW AGE:	CHRISTIANITY:
BECOME ALL THAT YOU CAN BE, empowered, because man is god.	BECOME ALL THAT YOU CAN BE because "I can do all things through Christ."
RESPECT FOR JESUS as a great person.	RESPECT FOR JESUS as a great person, and fully God.
HELP PEOPLE FEEL GOOD ABOUT THEMSELVES because there is no sin, only "mistakes."	HELP PEOPLE FEEL GOOD ABOUT THEMSELVES through confession of sin and God's forgiveness.

Children need to understand that New Age teaching and Christian teaching are opposite. Both cannot be true.

▶ WHAT THE BIBLE SAYS:

2 Timothy 4:3-4 The time will come when people will not listen to the true teaching. They will find more and more teachers who are pleasing to them, teachers who say the things they want to hear. They will stop listening to the truth. They will begin to follow the teaching in false stories.

2 Peter 2:1-2 And you will have some false teachers in your group. They will secretly teach things that are wrong—teachings that will cause people to be lost. They will even refuse to accept the Master, Jesus, who bought their freedom. And so they will quickly destroy themselves. Many will follow their evil ways and say evil things about the Way of truth.

▶ WHAT TO SAY:

"The Bible says that reincarnation is wrong. That's why we don't accept it. When people die, they either go to heaven or hell."

"Your mom and I have friends who believe in the New Age. One of

the ways non-Christians learn what the Bible really teaches is by friendships with Christians."

"The reason your mom and I don't let you watch that cartoon is because it has a character who is a 'spirit guide.'"

"Christians have always been people who are set apart. So, even if most of the people in our country believe in the New Age, there will always be Christians who believe only what the Bible teaches."

"Your dad and I are going to the parents' meeting at the school tonight so we can talk about the part of the curriculum that we feel is New Age teaching."

"The best way to be able to tell if something is true or not true is to know what the Bible says."

"You don't have to argue about your Christian beliefs, just say what you believe and why you believe it."

"The New Age is a religion that teaches that no one is a sinner in need of being saved. That's not what Jesus said."

"Some New Age beliefs are even in health care, such as therapeutic touch and the belief that everyone who is dying goes to a warm, accepting light. The Bible teaches that people who don't accept Christ will go to hell."

"God gives us guardian angels to protect us, not 'spirit guides.'"

[Also see: Do Good People Really Go to Hell?; Which Church Is Right?]

WHICH CHURCH IS RIGHT?

YOUNG CHILDREN assume that all churches teach the same thing. It is not until early grade school that children become aware that churches have different practices, although they still think that beliefs are the same in all churches. By the time children are in junior high, they usually have the ability to express the particular beliefs of their church.

Many adults cannot explain in a simple way how the beliefs of their church differ from other denominations or religions. Therefore, they are ill prepared to communicate this information to their children. Children whose parents have two distinctly different religious backgrounds are more able to teach their children the differences, for example, between Catholic and Baptist beliefs. For many Christian parents, the issue about what is essential to believe in order to be Christian, and what is simply a different emphasis of a particular church, is unclear.

What Children Need to Know:

- All religious groups are not the same, and in fact, many have teachings that are the opposite of beliefs of other churches.
- The guide for what is true is the Bible. The basic teaching about Christian faith is clearly stated in the Bible.
- Jesus Christ is not just equal to the leaders of the other

religions. Whenever other religions teach something that contradicts what the Bible teaches, the other religions are wrong.

- Churches that teach that Jesus was only a good man or a great teacher are wrong because Jesus said he is the one true God, the Creator of the universe, the only one who has never sinned. Jesus said that nobody can come to God except through Jesus and that he is the way and the truth.

- Children need to know that when we don't know what to believe, we can talk to God about this in prayer and that God's Holy Spirit will help us understand what is true.

- Children can be told that some people do not believe that Jesus is God (such as agnostics who do not know if there is a god), but lack of belief in God doesn't mean God is not real.

- Children learn basic Christian truth when:
    1. They have learned core Bible verses that tell about sin, Jesus' death and resurrection, man's sin and need for salvation, and how to live the Christian life.
    2. They observe their parents put into practice the teachings of the Bible.

- Children need to know that not all beliefs and practices are important. There is room for variety. Some churches emphasize one truth more than another church. Most people attend churches which are similar to the one they grew up in, or a church which seems to fit their family.

- There is no way to tell if a person is a Christian simply by which church he attends. Being a Christian is about following Christ.

▶ WHAT THE BIBLE SAYS:

John 14:6 Jesus answered, "I am the way. And I am the truth and the life. The only way to the Father is through me."

1 Corinthians 3:18-19 Do not fool yourselves. If anyone among you thinks he is wise in this world, he should become a fool. Then he can become truly wise, because the wisdom of this world is foolishness to God. It is written in the Scriptures, "He catches wise men in their own clever traps."

▶ WHAT TO SAY:

"The Bible says that God hears our prayers and answers them. Sometimes he says Yes, sometimes he says No, and sometimes he says Not yet. God knows what is best for us."

"Staying home from church in this family is not an option because we believe it is important to be with other Christians and worship together."

"Let's invite your Sunday school teacher to come over for dinner."

"Yes, you may go to your friend's church when you stay overnight with her, and then we can talk about some of the differences and similarities between that church and ours."

"Some common differences in belief in churches are: how to worship; whether babies should be baptized or only grown-ups; who is allowed to take communion; the role of women in church leadership; whether speaking in tongues is a part of Christian life today; and whether or not a person can lose their salvation after they become a Christian."

"Genuine Christians may understand the Bible differently."

"It isn't okay to argue or fight about different beliefs. Christians treat each other with respect and kindness."

[Also see: How Do I Know There Really Is a God?; New Age]

WHY BAD THINGS HAPPEN TO GOOD PEOPLE

What Children Might Experience:

BY THE time children are in first grade, they understand that some things are just not fair. Children believe they can control the circumstances of their lives by being good. When hardship or tragedy occurs, children seek someone or something to blame.

Children often determine that they are to blame for these unwanted events because of their angry thoughts or lack of obedience. They misinterpret statements of adults who fail to understand the danger of comments such as, "You are driving your mom crazy with your noise," or "If you don't sit quietly, Daddy will have a crash and everybody will be hurt." It is normal for young children to assume that the world rotates around them; that is, that they cause their parents to divorce, or grandpa to die. It is far too scary for the child to believe that random tragedy happens in the world. Children feel safe when there is a logical cause and effect. When a loved sister dies from cancer, the child cannot fathom that such a terrible thing could "just happen."

The child who grows up in a Christian home may have additional questions when he overhears adult conversations about

God's role in the event, such as, "If God is all powerful, couldn't he have stopped this from happening?" "Why doesn't God answer our prayers?" "Is God angry with us?" Children who have experienced tragedy will have more issues with why such events occur than children who have had few major difficulties. Sooner or later, all children will be touched by cruelty, disease, accident, or deep disappointment. Children commonly have simplistic solutions to these complex problems. Children will be deeply influenced by the response of their parents to hardship.

What Parents Can Do:

- Acknowledge honestly their own questions and confusion about why an event occurred. Parents can say, "We don't know why this happened"; or "You're right, it doesn't seem fair"; or "God doesn't get mad at us for saying how we feel."

- Tell children that God can be trusted, even when we don't understand.

- Say that we live in a world where bad things happen to good people because God has given us a choice about what we do (including doing dangerous things). Because we live in a sinful world, death and evil happen to bad people and good people alike.

- Remind children that in the beginning God made a perfect world that didn't have any hurts, but people chose to disobey God's plan. Someday, when we are in heaven, life will again be perfect.

- Encourage children to pray for people when they are sick and to ask God for protection when they are in danger. God hears and answers prayer.

- Tell children that Jesus understands what it is like to hurt because he was perfect and bad people killed him.

- Recognize that children need to know that God is stronger than evil and that he is not helpless, but he wants people to love and trust him even when they don't understand why bad things happen. If we only love God because he does good things for us, it isn't really love.

- Tell children that God wants Christians to do everything they

205

can to stop evil and pain in the world and to care about people who hurt.

- Inform children that people have choices about how they will respond to hurtful experiences. They can become bitter or they can grow. It is the person's choice.

- Acknowledge that sometimes when bad things happen, people come to God because they know they need him.

- Teach children that they can prevent many bad things from happening to them: for example, not smoking will decrease the possibility of getting lung cancer; wearing a helmet when they ride their bikes will prevent some injuries.

▶ WHAT THE BIBLE SAYS:

Ecclesiastes 9:1 I thought about something else and tried hard to understand it. I saw that God takes care of both good people and wise people and what they do. But no one knows if he will see good or bad times.

Matthew 5:45 Your Father causes the sun to rise on good people and on bad people. Your Father sends rain to those who do good and to those who do wrong.

▶ WHAT TO SAY:

"No, the rules are not the same for everyone in the family. Some privileges are earned by responsible behavior."

"It's not fair that your coach yells at you so much and never says what you are doing right. I know it is hard. One thing you can do is talk about your feelings at home. Can you think of anything else you can do to solve this problem?"

"I'm glad that you told me about the bully beating you up. I will go to school tomorrow and talk with the teacher about finding a way to keep you safe. This is an unfair situation that you cannot solve without help."

"Nobody did anything bad. The accident just happened because the streets were icy."

"God cares about our sad feelings right now."

"Christians help people who are having a hard time because that's what God told us to do."

"Someday when we are in heaven we can ask God all of our 'why' questions, and he will explain everything."

[Also see: Fears and Worries; How Do I Know There Really Is a God?; Natural Disasters]

OTHER BOOKS WRITTEN BY DORIS SANFORD FOR CHILDREN

ADOPTION:
> *Brian Was Adopted,* © 1989 Multnomah Press, Portland, Oregon. 28 pages (Children 5-9 yrs.) Video also available.

ALCOHOL:
> *I Know The World's Worst Secret,* © 1987 Multnomah Press, Portland, Oregon. 28 pages (Children 5-11 yrs.) Video also available.

CANCER:
> *No Longer Afraid,* © 1992 Questar Publishers, Inc., Post Office Box 1720, Sisters, Oregon 97759. 32 pages (Children 5-11 yrs.)

CEREBRAL PALSY:
> *Yes I Can,* © 1992 Questar Publishers, Inc., Post Office Box 1720, Sisters, Oregon 97759. 32 pages (Children 5-11 yrs.)

CONFLICT:
> *Lisa's Parents Fight,* © 1989 Multnomah Press, Portland, Oregon. 31 pages (Children 5-9 yrs.) Video also available.

DEATH:
> *It Must Hurt A Lot,* © 1985 Multnomah Press, Portland, Oregon. 32 pages (Children 5-11 yrs.) Video also available.

DEMENTIA:
> *Maria's Grandma Gets Mixed Up,* © 1989 Multnomah Press, Portland, Oregon. 31 pages (Children 5-9 yrs.) Video also available.

DEPRESSION:
> *It Won't Last Forever,* © 1993 Questar Publishers, Inc., Post Office Box 1720, Sisters, Oregon 97759. 32 pages (Children 5-11 yrs.)

DISABILITY:
> *Help! Fire!* © 1992 Questar Publishers, Inc., Post Office Box 1720, Sisters, Oregon 97759. 32 pages (Children 5-11 yrs.)

DIVORCE:
> *Please Come Home,* © 1985 Multnomah Press, Portland, Oregon. 32 pages (Children 5-11 yrs.) Video also available.

DRUG ABUSE:
> *I Can Say No,* © 1987 Multnomah Press, Portland, Oregon. 32 pages (Children 5-11 yrs.) Video also available.

FOSTER CARE:
> *For Your Own Good,* © 1993 Questar Publishers, Inc., Post Office Box 1720, Sisters, Oregon 97759. 32 pages (Children 5-11 yrs.)

PRISON CAMP:
> *My Friend The Enemy,* © 1992 Questar Publishers, Inc., Post Office Box 1720, Sisters, Oregon 97759. 32 pages (Children 5-11 yrs.)

RITUAL ABUSE:
> *Don't Make Me Go Back, Mommy,* © 1990 Multnomah Press, Portland, Oregon. 32 pages (Children 5-11 yrs.)

SELF-ESTEEM:

Don't Look At Me, © 1986 Multnomah Press, Portland, Oregon. 27 pages (Children 5-11 yrs.) Video also available.

SEX ABUSE (Boy):

Something Must Be Wrong With Me, © 1993 Questar Publishers, Inc., Post Office Box 1720, Sisters, Oregon 97759. 32 pages (Children 5-11 yrs.)

SEX ABUSE (Girl):

I Can't Talk About It, © 1986 Multnomah Press, Portland, Oregon. 32 pages (Children 5-11 yrs.) Audio tape and video also available.

STEPPARENT:

My Real Family, © 1993 Questar Publishers, Inc., Post Office Box 1720, Sisters, Oregon 97759. 32 pages (Children 5-11 yrs.)

For a catalog write to:

Heart to Heart, Inc.
2115 S.E. Adams Street
Milwaukie, Oregon 97222
(503) 654-3870

INDEX

ABOUT THE AUTHOR

Doris Sanford grew up in China with her missionary parents. She became a widow at age thirty when her husband fell while mountain climbing, leaving her with two preschool children. The children are grown now, and Doris lives with a large dog in a small cottage near the river in a suburb of Portland, Oregon.

Professionally, Doris is a consultant to her home state Children's Services Division where she assesses abused children who live in foster care. In addition, she speaks about children's issues throughout North America. *How to Answer Tough Questions Kids Ask* is Doris's twenty-ninth book.

All of her free time is spent sitting on the floor playing with her grandson.